UNFUSSY LIFE

Copyright © 2021 by Jacqueline Fisch

All rights reserved.

No part of this book may be reproduced in any form or by any electronic or mechanical means, including information storage and retrieval systems, without written permission from the author, except for the use of brief quotations in a book review.

978-1-7365542-0-3 (hardcover)
978-1-7365542-1-0 (paperback)
978-1-7365542-2-7 (ebook)

UNFUSSY LIFE

An Intuitive Approach to Navigating Change

JACQUELINE FISCH

UNFUSSY LIFE

An Intuitive Approach to Navigating Change

JACQUELINE FISCH

Copyright © 2021 by Jacqueline Fisch

All rights reserved.

No part of this book may be reproduced in any form or by any electronic or mechanical means, including information storage and retrieval systems, without written permission from the author, except for the use of brief quotations in a book review.

978-1-7365542-0-3 (hardcover)
978-1-7365542-1-0 (paperback)
978-1-7365542-2-7 (ebook)

For you. May you find magic in the messy middle.

And for my mostly unfussy family, Ryan, Jacob, and Talia.

Contents

Introduction — xi

I. LEARNING ABOUT CHANGE IN CHILDHOOD

You're too young to drink beer	3
All the chocolate, all the presents	10
Bite your cheeks to stop the tears	14
New city, new school, new house	19
I'm leaving	26

II. CHOOSING CHANGE IN MY TWENTIES

I want to be rich and famous, but only if it's easy	33
It's not you, it's me	37
Finding love in a dive bar	40
Meeting American strangers in the woods	45
I wrote you something	50
That's Miss Canada to you	56
The interview that would determine our fate	60
Opening the floodgates for more expansive change	63

III. RIDING THE CHAOS CRAZY TRAIN

Why am I puking so much?	71
The birth unplan	74
Pipes work!	77
Growing pains	81
Untrying a third time	86

IV. EMBRACING THE UNFUSSY LIFE

Death bothers us because it reminds us of our own mortality	93
Good things in all kinds of packages	99

Less stuff, more life	108
Honey, I threw out the bacon	114
Sneaking shrimps over the kitchen stove	118
When life hands you a shit-sicle	124
I see you	128
Slow slow slow the holidays	132
Belonging nowhere and nowhere	138

V. GOING ALL-IN ON ME

Dismissed	145
No one is layoff proof	153
Screw your well-roundedness	156
Creating a life I don't need a vacation from	161
I quit!	165
Slow the fuck down	168
Not my circus, not my monkeys	173
Our thoughts are a shitty boss	178
You've got a masterpiece to create	181
Motivation isn't the problem	186
What do you want to be known for?	189

VI. TRUSTING MY INTUITION

They're here to suck your blood	195
Drink the good wine	202
Watch the damn sunset	207
There's no prize for being the most social	210
Being okay with messy me	217
A different kind of diet	222
The busy trap	228
Rest is a verb	233
FOMO is a bitch	241
The secret to having time is protecting it like a MOFO	245
Meditation my way	250
Spiritual labor	255
Un-random acts of gratitude	259
They knew it all along, but I finally woke up	264

Outro	271
Gratitude	275
Epilogue	276
About the Author	279
About The Intuitive Writing School Community	281

Introduction

How do you measure your life?

I've seen the musical *Rent* three times — New York, Chicago, and Toronto. I've also watched the movie more times than I can count.

In the musical, there's a song that sums up the minutes of our lives — "Seasons of Love." Five-hundred twenty-five thousand, six hundred minutes (525,600). This represents the number of minutes in a year. How do you measure your year? Like the song suggests, with cups of coffee, dollars, contracts, funerals, and births?

Or sunsets, miles, laughter, and strife? This all feels so squishy.

There's one standard measurement for life, and that's love.

I used to hear this song and feel pain. A wrench would turn in my gut because I wasn't living the life I wanted. I was making everyone else happy and racking up promotions, debt, and crap I didn't need. All measures of success that, while they look impressive on paper, left me feeling empty.

I needed change. When I pressed pause to turn my phone off, sit down, and look around, I hardly recognized my life. I don't want this to happen to you.

This is a book about change. About accepting and navigating it when it's hurled your way and choosing it when you're looking for something different than what you currently have.

This book is an invitation. To savor not only the first sip of coffee but the tenth and the last. To start noticing things you may not have seen before. To start paying attention. To take back control of your life and start living it like you mean it.

It took me years to figure out the changes I needed and a cadence that works for my life. I've learned some lessons many times over. This rhythm of intentional transformation will continue to evolve.

Change is inevitable, so when you have the opportunity to guide it along or point it in the direction you want it to go, take it.

Change happens whether we want it or not. What we do know for sure is that we get the change we need. Sometimes that's not the easiest thing to accept.

I hope this book encourages you to think about the changes you've experienced and created throughout your life. There might be more than you think. And if you're thinking about a change, maybe this book will be the nudge you need.

Cause a ruckus. Stir shit up. Dye your hair purple. You've got one life. This book will show you how to take an unfussy approach to life by embracing and creating change.

To live a fussy life means to experience the world like a colicky baby. One who whines and can't quite get comfortable. Never really happy, always fussing. The adult version of this looks a lot like the complaining grown-up — never satisfied, always needing something different, discontented with everything all the time.

Unfussy is the opposite. It doesn't mean you're a pushover or get walked all over. It means you put the whining and complaining down, drop the suitcase, and be here now.

Be here. Be in your life. Be the person you're proud of while you make changes in your life for the better.

I've written this book to show you how I navigated this in my own life. It's organized into six tidy parts.

I. Learning about Change in Childhood.

Here's where I'll give you a personal tour through growing up as a first-generation Canadian in suburban Toronto. It was all about the status quo until my grandparents died within fifteen months of each other, creating a cascade of change.

II. Choosing Change in My Twenties.

Two decades in, we have to make some big choices that will affect the rest of our lives. Here, you'll learn about how I took the easy road when I had the option. My life was pretty boring until I clinked Corona bottles with a tattooed New Yorker at last call in a dingy Florida bar.

III. Riding the Chaos Crazy Train.

Babies are fussy. It's their job to come in like a hurricane and toss all our best laid plans out the window, thinking, "That's cute."

IV. Embracing the Unfussy Life.

Unfussy is a destination, and I'm still on the journey. You'll never see me pretending I've "made it." Here, you'll see how I navigated moving eleven times in sixteen years, going vegan and back, and losing myself in becoming who I thought I was supposed to be.

V. Going All-In on Me.

Who gets laid off three times in five years? And, twice from the same company? That'd be me. Call me a slow learner, but this is where I cracked open and turned my back on all things "familiar" and "safe" to start listening to my gut.

VI. Trusting my Intuition.

This is where shit really gets wild. I unlocked a new part of my brain that was previously asleep. Relentlessly focused and finally listening to those nudges, I cut out the bullshit, learned how to sit with my thoughts, and most importantly, stopped apologizing.

You're about to go on a journey through change with me.

Through my childhood eyes to making fast decisions in my twenties, to riding a shit storm of chaos, leading me to ultimately make an inward turn, and get comfortable being me.

It's that inward turn that taught me how to trust myself and share this unfussy life advice with you. I'm the one who's responsible for my journey, and I can navigate the inevitable ups and downs with grace.

You're a beautiful soul and should never change.

Unless you want to.

I. LEARNING ABOUT CHANGE IN CHILDHOOD

"Change is inevitable. Growth is optional."

John C. Maxwell

We learn how to be in the world based on what we see. I saw people working hard, choosing big changes, and choosing to simply be. I'd end up with a life that was in some ways wildly different from that of many of my ancestors, and in some ways, exactly the same. No one did it "right" or "wrong" — we did, and are doing, the best we can with what we know.

You're too young to drink beer

I never really thought about digging into my past to look at how I grew up until I started hearing stories of strife, struggle, and sadness from others. When I first wandered over to the self-development section of the bookstore, I discovered many stories of trial and trauma. In one book after another, people were experiencing the lowest of lows and then taking the reader on a journey to complete transformation.

Their stories weren't my stories.

I don't need to get into the details of these specific stories, but the theme in all of them was that they'd all been through some super shitty stuff — abuse, anger, loss, death. Even as I'd gather with new friends, I'd find the ones who appeared to have their shit the most together were the ones who were the quickest to fall apart after two vodka and tonics. As one would start to shed her tears, friends to the left and right of her would rub her arm in an attempt to comfort her. And then, one by one, they'd all empathize — "Me too," "I get it," "I've been there."

Every time I heard their stories, I thought, *Wow, that's terrible; I'm glad that didn't happen to me.* And then I'd sit there with a stupid look on my face, listening as best I could, nodding along, and letting them know I saw them, saying things like "That must have been so hard," and "I can't imagine."

I didn't have these same stories of pain and sadness to share. I couldn't say "me too" without lying. I felt like I was different. Boring and not dramatic enough. My stories paled in comparison. And somehow because I grew up in middle-class Toronto suburbia, I believed I didn't have a story worth telling.

Even the idea of diving into these stories in 2020 brings up uncomfortable questions. *Who am I to tell my story? Am I recognizing my privilege only after being reminded of it? Comparing my stories to others, are they small? Who even cares? Do I have anything important to say here?*

While deep in revisions of this book, while that inner voice still whispered in my ear, "no one wants to read your stories," I had a dream that shook me awake. My heart pounding, I looked around the room to make sure I was still alive.

In the dream, I was attempting to speak. Except the words didn't come. I opened my mouth — and nothing. Now, I've had plenty of dreams about losing teeth and walking into class without pants (more than I care to admit), but the no-voice thing — this was new.

I remember opening my mouth, and when the words wouldn't come, I'd grasp my throat, eyes wide in horror. I couldn't speak. At that moment, I realized that not speaking up meant dying.

And next, I started shrinking into bed and through the floor, sinking into death, where I'd cease to exist.

Then I woke up, saw Ryan in bed, and realized it was all a dream.

Staying silent wasn't something new for me (I was no stranger to silence).

Speak when you're spoken to.

If you don't have anything nice to say, don't say anything at all.

You'll make them mad if you say that.

You need to do whatever it takes to make people like you.

Everyone will see you. And when they notice you, you're opening yourself up for judgment.

I put this book down for three months around the time of that dream.

Others have suffered more than me, others have suffered less. It might be a stretch to say I've even suffered at all.

I can't let someone else tell my story. I am the only one who can tell my story. Even when it's hard — and especially when it's uncomfortable. And it's almost always uncomfortable.

I'll start my story where my parents began filling in the blanks. I'm a first-generation Canadian. My dad, born in the Azores, on a small island, São Miguel, immigrated to Canada with his mom, dad, and older brother when he was just two years old (and his younger brother was born several years later in Canada). He doesn't remember life in Portugal other than what his parents told him and from only a trip or two back to the motherland. We did, however, hear repeatedly about the Portuguese donkeys. "There are donkeys everywhere!" my dad would often declare.

My *vavô* (my grandfather) moved to Canada an entire year before relocating the family. He landed in British Columbia, and then when he brought the rest of the family over, they landed in a Toronto suburb — Streetsville, their neighbors being the others who came from their village.

Early memories of being at my dad's parents' mostly involved food — lots and lots of food. My *vavó* (my grandmother) loved to feed everyone.

The first sentences I learned to say in Portuguese were "I'm full — *estou cheio*" and "I have a belly ache — *dors de barriga*." Key phrases to master unless you wanted to walk around with your pants unbuttoned all evening.

Vavó's response, "You no eat? You no love me?"

I would think, ah, fine, okay, I'm throwing up in my mouth, but I'll cram another glorious red peppery roasted potato down my throat — if it's to prove my love to you, after all, I'll do it. I mean, they are delicious.

From an early age, I began to associate food and love. If you love others, you eat their food. And the more you eat, the more you like them. Often to the point of running over to the couch to lie down because there was no energy left to do anything else besides digest dinner.

The only thing my vavó loved more than her family and food was Jesus. Baby Jesus, adult Jesus, Jesus on the cross — there was a lot of love to go around for Jesus. Jesus was all over the house. My sister and I referred to my grandparents' bedroom as the "Jesus room" because it was the room in the house with the most Jesuses. As a kid, the Jesus room was kind of scary. Glowing sculptures set on top of thick mahogany furniture, a matching altar, enough rosaries for anyone who'd be willing to pray with her, statues, posters, bibles. We used to dare each other to peek into the room, never touching a thing because… Jesus!

My vavó's English was never super strong, though as I got older, I wondered how she'd lived in Canada for seventy years and didn't manage to pick up the language. I have a pretty good hunch that she knew exactly what we were saying most of the time and just got to smile and nod while people were talking about her. Everyone so smug as they talked about her, thinking she had no clue — I knew better, she was smart.

She lived the ultimate minimalist life before minimalism was cool. She didn't drive, work, or do much else other than visit church daily, pray, have friends over, and cook. She had *a lot* of friends. As an adult, I wonder how she had so many friends. I guess when your entire Portuguese village moves to your town and your primary role is to look after your family, then you have plenty of time to stay connected with your people.

People stopped by their house all the time. Every time we were there, they welcomed at least a few uninvited (and always welcome) guests. There was always enough food — just in case.

She had way more friends in her eighties and nineties than

I've had my entire life. I wonder if this is why she was so bright and full of love. I remember her presiding at the kitchen table with her friends, sipping tea and room temperature water, offering around a tin of shortbread cookies.

Vavó had two prominent love languages — food and physical affection. If you wanted simply to sit and hug her all day long, she'd be in all her glory. Only breaking up the love fest for some *pastéis de nata* (Portuguese custard tarts) and *massa* (sweet bread).

My vavô was always doing some kind of work. I don't remember him leaving to go to an actual job, though he worked at the Ford plant, but I do remember him tending to his pigeon coop (and later welcoming canaries to the flock). I loved running between the perfectly manicured bushes that lined the concrete pathway from the house to the coop.

The coop smelled like bird shit. Literally, because there were so many dang birds there. My sister, Jen, and I danced down the walkway as if it were our own personal fashion runway. We'd help out and feed the birds or just walk through and look at them. I remembered walking through there with my dad, and my vavô would want to show off his latest birds. They all looked the same to me. Except the birds of a different color — he'd feed them special food to get them to change color — red, blue, green.

Something I didn't care a whole lot about at the time.

What I did care a lot about later on was the beer and wine. My vavô made his own beer and wine (moonshine too — I later discovered he was a shine runner in Toronto for thirty years). I'd smell the moonshine cap and dry heave, so I never ventured into actually putting that stuff in my mouth. On the occasional bee sting or bug bite, sure, but that stuff was better suited for *outside* the body. And I'm guessing my parents would have probably been charged with child abuse if they'd let me taste it.

At ten years old, I recall a Christmas Eve when after dinner we gathered at the next-door neighbor's house. You know, because after you stuff your face with Christmas Eve stewed shrimp, seafood, potatoes, and bread, you eat dessert and then go to a neighbor's house to eat some more.

Jokingly, the neighbor, who we called Mr. Gilbert, offered me a beer. He quickly changed his mind and said, "No, you're too young for beer, have some liquor," as he poured me a delicate glass of liquid diabetes that tasted like peaches.

At that age, I was allowed to have a small glass of wine at dinner. It was a dinner staple. I felt oh so grown-up sipping red table wine. I didn't really brag about it to my friends though. I thought it was normal — you drink wine with dinner, that's how it's supposed to be.

Until some of my friends started drinking in high school and had to steal booze from their parents. While I was like, "Why would you do that? I drink wine with dinner at my grandparents' house; why would I need to sneak it to drink more?"

When my grandparents immigrated to Canada, they made a huge change. Trading a lush, colorful, island life for one less vibrant. They kept their language, prepared the food they'd always made, and kept the same company. They made the ultimate change so that much of their lives could stay the same.

Looking at their lives from the outside, I saw how much a thread of sameness ran through them. We ate the same handful of foods (which I wasn't mad about), followed a similar routine every time we visited — go say hi to Vavó working in the kitchen, wander outside to the coop to say *olá* to Vavô, then to the basement (all the Portuguese people I know hang out in the basement) to crunch Corn Nuts, nibble on shrimp cocktail, and chips with onion dip. Every single time. Until dinner when we'd tread back upstairs and buckle in for more face-stuffing.

Vavó visited church every single day. I'm not sure this was about a lack of wanting to change things, but what about skipping church on Tuesday to go to Friday night mass — you know, live it up a little?

After Vavô died, we asked Vavó about a potential family trip to Portugal, but she adamantly shook her head. "No, no, no, it's too sad there." She left the country seventy years before. We tried to explain that things changed and are different there now, but she had zero interest. Streetsville, Ontario was her home now and that was perfectly fine with her.

Was she afraid of changing up her routine from her everyday life to travel back to the motherland? Or was it the idea of a changed homeland that had her opting for staying put? I'm not sure what was motivating her to want to avoid changing her scenery to travel. Anytime I've traveled back to a former vacation spot or home, yeah, it changes — every single time. *Why'd they tear down the family restaurant to build more condos?* Maybe seeing a place we love in a new light messes with our memories. We want to preserve things a certain way — or perhaps forget them. Digging our heels in, we don't even want to go there. And I wonder if this is how my grandmother felt about visiting her homeland.

Was life unfussier for them in Portugal or in Canada? Was Vavó choosing what felt better for her, in that moment? Was her perception of Portugal not as colorful as I imagined, and life in Canada was the one that stood out to her as easier and friendlier? I'll never know.

Later in my life, when I went on my own immigration adventures, I look back to their experiences and I realize — I was built for this. Embracing ultimate change is in my blood and in the memories of my cells.

All the chocolate, all the presents

There were many constants in my life up until I hit the double digits. We spent two weeks each summer driving four hours north of Toronto up to a Northern Ontario cottage on a quiet little lake, often traveling with my Canadian grandparents — Grampa and Gramma, as we called them. My mom and dad would drive up to meet us a week later.

I spent a lot of time alone with my grandparents at Wolfe Lake. Finding the perfect walking stick for nature walks with my gramma, boat rides and fishing with both of them, looking to catch glimpses of the loon, and lots of card games — it's where I learned how to play crazy eights.

The one-on-one time I had with my grandparents, sans sister and parents, were some of my favorite times. My sister and I had lots of fun together when we were little. With three years in between us, we had our share of Barbie and Nintendo playing, but as an introvert, sometimes I just needed some alone time.

We'd drive up to the lake early on a July Saturday morning in my grampa's 1981 green Oldsmobile, eating chocolate chip cookies the whole way. My gramma would talk to everyone. I remember her constant singing and offering cookies to the gas station attendants.

We'd spend many days just putzing around the cabin in the woods, playing on the sand while the teeny waves lapped the shore. It was a small lake, and you could quickly boat from one side to the other. Right after attaching the old motor to the wooden boat and joking, "Maybe this'll be the year it doesn't start." That thing had to be fifty years old when *I* was a kid. Who knows when it actually died. We loved heading out on the paddle boats, collecting lily pads, listening to the loons, catching frogs, and sitting around watching an old TV on rainy days. These activities filled a good chunk of our summers.

If the Toronto Blue Jays game wasn't on, the radio was. My gramma was the only one who had a musical bone in her body, and I'm pretty sure she kept all that talent to herself. Experts say it's statistically improbable to be part of the tone-deaf population; I'm pretty sure I'm part of that percentage. She'd sing, play piano, and dance around — and I enjoyed watching and listening, but never once thought, *I wish I could do that.*

I tried to learn to play the piano from her one time. As she grabbed my fingers and fanned them out across her electric organ, she commented on how I had piano-playing hands. Even though that left me feeling pretty special, I'd later feel frustrated when I couldn't manipulate the same sounds out of the organ as she did.

To be fair, she'd hear a tune, trod over to the organ, and be able to sit down and play it. Pure grace, and well, that was also her name — Grace.

My grampa (or "Pompa" as I called him when I was too young to form the right sounds) was quieter. He'd keep mostly to himself, always appearing content to be sitting and watching his grandkids play. I remember his silliness and generous personality. He was a giver — you could count on him to deliver various denominations of cash out of his big fat wallet and to pick us up from school every Thursday, with three full-sized candy bars for each of us. We'd eat at least two of them in one sitting when we returned home.

It's no wonder my chubby phase lasted into college, and I eat chocolate every single day now. Most households make sure they're well-stocked with toilet paper — mine, chocolate. Most days, I'll enjoy a square or two from a really great dark bar after lunch, and a few more after dinner.

It's interesting looking back on those regular Thursdays, knowing exactly what to expect every week. Our weeks often revolved around those candy-filled days. How many days left until Thursday?

My mom grew up and later returned to the same city where she was born. An only child, she often referred to being spoiled, which didn't suck when my sister and I arrived. Being the only grandchildren, birthdays and holidays bordered on excessive, and I can't imagine buying that much crap for my kids today.

There were years when the Christmas presents were piled halfway up the tree. And on birthdays, it would take hours to open all the gifts. Even the sibling who didn't have a birthday still got loads of presents. You know, in case we'd feel left out or something. God forbid we sat by and watched each other open gifts and felt happy for each other. Instead, we got our own bag, unwrapped, filled with just as many toys. Another habit I kept in my childhood container and didn't introduce to my kids. By the time we had two kids — and seeing how much stuff they accumulated without looking and didn't use — I wasn't going to teach them to start to expect presents for every occasion. As an adult, I get to choose which patterns I learned in childhood that I'll consciously follow, and those I'll leave behind.

I look back at some of those habits that I deemed as "bad" and think, *I'm going to do better.* And I recognize that everyone is really doing the best job they can with what they know in the moment.

And on the other hand, sometimes getting three chocolate bars a week and a truckload of presents gets old. We find ourselves restless, and then we make a change just for change's sake. Which, if you're wondering, is a perfectly good reason to change.

We spent a lot of time with my mom and her parents growing up. A stay-at-home mom for the first ten years of my life, she was the one that got us to school, all our appointments, and did all the shopping, cooking, and cleaning. She looked after everything while my dad was at work nearby as a mechanic in an auto repair shop.

My Portuguese grandparents taught me about resisting change and the importance of holding onto familiar and cherished foods and customs. My Canadian grandparents taught me about the pleasures of embracing routines.

Now, from where I sit, I've chosen a certain degree of change that my parents didn't. And I know this is my perception. They weren't thinking the same thoughts about change that I am today. All this change comes with lots of benefits — living in different states, moving when the mood strikes and the job is right — but it also has some drawbacks. My kids won't get the constancy of all their grandparents in their lives the way I did. Now that I live an eight-hour drive away from my family, my kids will never get to experience the gift of a regular, 3:00 p.m. sugarcoated visit from any grandparent.

Bite your cheeks to stop the tears

I have many memories from when I was a young child of us doing stuff together as a family — just my mom, dad, sister, and me. We'd take trips to the zoo, the lake cottage, and the Florida Gulf Coast. My parents loved the predictability and ease of visiting the same places during summer and spring break: same city, same motel on the beach, same cabin, same route to get there. We'd even visit the same restaurants, almost in the same order, with every visit — why take a chance and eat something you don't like and have it potentially ruin your meal?

Predictability is queen. The only time I recall trying a new restaurant on vacation was if we'd received a raving recommendation from someone we trusted. This often landed us at obscure Italian restaurants in strip malls — and they often ended up being the best meals. There would always be a nonna serving up extra helpings of spaghetti with Bolognese, which I could eat three days a week — and growing up, I often did.

Extraordinary change wasn't woven into my growing-up experience. Sure, when my sister was born just before my third birthday, she shook things up. I went from being the only child, getting all the attention and presents, to having to share all my toys and clothes, and even my identity to the extent that my clothes were a part of who I was. Birthdays and all holidays were an opportunity for them to spoil us with matching outfits. They thought it was cute; I resented every second.

Other than that, having a sister meant that I had the opportunity to have someone to look after, and later a live-in friend to play Barbies with. My mom later told me how I loved to "check" on her when she was a baby. In one of these "checks," she supposedly caught me reaching down into the crib and squeezing my sister's fat head. I have no recollection.

The most significant and notable change in our lives growing up was when Gramma and Grampa got cancer and passed away — within fifteen months of each other. It was a change that none of us would have chosen — *you get cancer, and you get cancer.*

My mom is an only child, and their deaths shook her world in a way that I'll never be able to comprehend fully. The loneliness she must have felt, with no siblings there to hold each other up and help each other through.

The changes started happening when my grampa was diagnosed with colon cancer at the age of fifty-three. At the lake with them the summer before his diagnosis, I felt guilty for not spending enough time with him. I turned down a third round of playing crazy eights with him in favor of going tubing on the lake with the cabin owner and the other kids.

My grampa thought being whipped around the lake behind a speedboat was stupid and dangerous. And I was intrigued — I was nine at the time. I remember walking down to the dock that morning, feeling the weight of guilt that I had left him alone in the cabin. I felt pulled in different directions. I wanted to go outside and have fun on the lake, and I also wanted to sit at the kitchen table, by the window, looking at the lake through the pines. He never said anything that led me to believe he was angry. These ideas lived in my head.

Early that December, when we got the news of his diagnosis, my mind instantly flashed back to that moment where I chose high-speed water sports over slow card-playing. The diagnosis came quickly, and when the surgeons got in there to try to remove the cancer, they discovered that it had spread to his liver and lungs. It was too late.

On the day of his surgery, my mom waited by the clunky beige phone in our townhome's basement for the news from her mom. My sister, dad, and I were all upstairs, vegging out in front of the television when we heard her slam the receiver down. She bolted up the stairs in tears. "It spread to his lungs, it's too late."

At ten, this was my first introduction to someone close to me being sick and close to death. My mom did the best she could to prepare my sister and I for the changes while managing her grief.

"Things are going to be different with Grampa now. You have to remember all the good stuff that's happened up until this point. Okay? Can you promise to focus on the fun times?"

Not totally sure what we were committing to exactly, we agreed.

He was only in the hospital for a few days to recover from surgery, and then was sent home.

I filled the next two weeks with visits. Grampa would be sitting in his recliner, which was his normal spot in healthy days, but now he was losing weight rapidly, shrinking in the chair, and his skin was turning yellow as his organs began shutting down. We'd try to have a "normal" visit, and it was all so weird. I didn't know how to act. How do you act around someone who's dying, and knows it? One morning, four days after Christmas and just twenty days after his surgery, we got the call we'd been anticipating from my grandmother. "He's getting really close." My dad drove us the twenty minutes to their townhome in the next town, dropped my mom off, and drove my sister and me back home.

My mom, my gramma, and the nurse were with him when he passed. After he died, my dad drove us *back* to their house and took us directly into the basement with him so that we wouldn't see my grampa's body. We were joined by my mom and gramma when the funeral home people arrived. We waited down there until the coast was clear.

Normally, the basement was a fun place for us to play. We'd spend hours getting lost in endless Pac-Man games on the Atari, cycling in imaginary races on the stationary bike, and playing with my gramma's antiques. Occasionally we came across an old *Playboy* magazine of my grampa's. This time, the basement didn't feel like a fun adventure. My sister and I, seven and ten, sat there, a mixed bag of nerves and nosiness, half playing with our Barbies and half straining to hear what was going on upstairs.

What does death sound like? What did he look like? We were completely clueless.

At the time, I wasn't mad and later wondered why death had to be this thing to hide. I had no idea what to expect. I was curious about death. *What happens when you die? Why is this a secret? Why am I too young to be with my grampa when he dies?*

What followed was a series of firsts — first visit inside a funeral home, discussions about caskets and funeral costs, a viewing, eulogies, a funeral, a burial, and grief.

I remember my mom saying to me the morning of the funeral service, "If you bite your cheek from the inside, you'll stop the tears. That's what I do."

I wondered, *Why do I need to stop the tears? Oh, we need to hide our crying — crying is bad.*

I learned to bite the insides of my cheek hard. So hard that I'd later notice the grooves with my tongue. It's a habit I still sometimes go back to when I'm fighting back tears in public — like when we're in a restaurant, and I don't want to cause a scene or attract any attention.

Later, all my relatives would comment on how strong I was.

The result of rigid, sore cheeks, but I was strong, and strength was something people admire.

Okay, so the lesson I learned as a child: It's important to minimize death, which is ultimately, the most final change of all. Especially don't be present for it — hide in the basement if you can, and then when you're feeling sad, definitely don't cry in public — someone might see you.

We began a different life and tried to get back to a new normal. There was the time when we had our Canadian grandparents and the time when they were gone.

New city, new school, new house

Just fifteen months after my grampa died, my gramma followed him. People said she literally died of a broken heart. She had fought a battle with breast cancer at the age of forty-eight, just five years earlier, and was in remission — until year five, and it was back.

As soon as the quietness settled in after my grampa's funeral, what followed was another year of hospital visits, making friends with some of my gramma's hospital roommates, such as Mrs. Stephanie, an old lady we'd play cards with, and then, her passing at home.

The day she died, my mom had driven out there by herself for what she thought was just a regular visit on a Sunday. She later told me she knew she was getting close but didn't think it would be that day. It was just the nurse and my mom there, and the nurse had repositioned her to her side to check a bedsore, rolled her back, and then she took her last breaths a few minutes later.

It was unexpected from the point of it happening so soon. She called my dad after, and he drove out with my sister and me — and again, we went back down to the basement since her body was still in the living room.

It was a rinse repeat of Pac-Man eating dots while we waited for the coast to clear and learn that it was "safe" to come upstairs — as in, no more dead bodies here.

Being at my gramma and grampa's house without them was eerie. Both of them were gone now, and I didn't want to be there. There was no reason to be there. For almost two years, we spent much of our extra time bouncing around from a mint-green hospital room to their home and back, and now what do we do?

We had adjusted to life without my grampa, and now there was another adjustment. We were just getting the hang of things it seemed.

After my gramma died, my mom, being an only child, inherited everything. And when I say "everything," I'm not talking about the keys to the castle and all the riches in the world. At the time, it felt like a lot of money. And, being eleven years old, I didn't have much of a concept of money except that my parents fought about it a lot and said things like "money doesn't grow on trees," "money brings out the worst in people," or "money is the devil."

Suddenly, with a few signatures and some bank transfers, money was no longer a problem for our family. Maybe this meant my mom and dad would stop arguing about it. Maybe we could finally stop shopping at Kmart and have nice clothes so we could fit in with the stylish kids at school.

With the proceeds of the sale of my grandparents' home, plus their savings, we moved out of our rented townhome, one town over into a four-bedroom house that, at 2,500 square feet, seemed like a mansion. Shopping for a new home was fun. My sister and I would race up the stairs and choose our bedrooms right away, and in the days that followed, I'd imagine how I'd do life in that home.

I'd picture where I'd set my backpack by the front door when I got off the school bus, and the path I'd walk to the kitchen for a snack. I'd then imagine myself walking the stairs to my bedroom, where I'd spend the late afternoon listening to the radio and trying to record songs on my boombox without the DJ ruining it before dinner.

Moving to a new home was a fun and exciting change. It was going to a new school in the seventh grade that was almost as unexciting as those hospital visits. Of all the times to change schools, seventh grade might be the most awkward. High school is right up there too, but at least there are more kids to help you blend in.

Going into seventh grade, I'd celebrate my twelfth birthday later that month. Switching schools during puberty shouldn't be allowed. Here's me — oily, developing, newly menstruating, tallest girl in my class — changing schools. I don't even know who I am anymore. I'm too old to play with Barbies and too young to do teenage things. My brain is fighting to cling to childhood where it's safe and familiar, and my body is pushing me toward becoming a teenager — with hips and boobs! Ack! The pressure to fit in at this age was intense. What would these new people wear? Would I make friends? Would I make a single friend, or would this be where I'd embrace the loserdom that I so feared?

Up through sixth grade, I'd lived in the same house, and went to the same school with the same group of friends since kindergarten. A new kid or two would join our class every now and again, and I remember looking at the new kid and worrying about them taking my place. Worrying that my current circle of friends would find out that I really was a loser after all, and they'd trade me in for the new girl. Of course, that's never what actually happened.

Why did we have to move anyway? Why did we need a bigger house in another town? Everything was fine where we were. We moved a few weeks before the school year ended, and my parents had us finish the year at our old school — I was grateful for that. My sixth-grade teacher happened to live near our new house, so he drove my sister and I to and from school each day for two weeks. I liked my teacher and all, but driving fifteen minutes with him after staring at him and listening to him talk all day wasn't exactly my idea of a relaxing ride home. At least I got to finish out the school year with a going-away party, surrounded by my friends.

We had the summer in our new home — where I made neighborhood friends pretty easily. We'd ride bikes, go to the park, or spend the whole day whizzing around our neighborhood on inline skates. These friends were cool and all, but when I asked what school they went to, they all went to the local public school. My sister and I were going to Catholic school.

In Ontario, Catholic school is considered part of the public-school system. You just direct your taxes differently. I could almost count the number of times we went to church as a family outside of weddings and funerals. Since my dad came from a very Catholic family (my vavó had a Jesus room, remember?) and my mom didn't have any religious preference other than celebrating the usual Hallmark holidays, they wanted to raise my sister and I Catholic. Which meant going through the motions of the sacraments — baptism as babies, first confession and communion in the second grade, and confirmation in the eighth grade. We didn't pray at home, except when I begged God to let me get my first period at home (I didn't), and to be able to transition to this new school gracefully and make friends (I didn't).

I was nervous and remembered that everyone already knew one another — the knew-one-another-since-preschool kind of knowing. I was the new kid. This was when I remembered more than ever how very hard I tried to fit in. I became overly conscious of how uncool my clothes were, and even my binders and backpack — how did I always choose the *wrong* things at the store? Mustard-yellow jeans, maroon bodysuits, Doc Martens, and shimmery vests — I saw lots of my classmates wearing these things, so I needed to wear them too.

I felt like an outsider — and I *was* an outsider. I was the new kid with no history of being with these kids. I wish I could say that the school year got easier once I wiggled my way into the cool crowd — it didn't. That year stands out as one of the most awkward and uncomfortable years of my life, and puberty sure didn't help.

I connected with one friend, Shana, early in the year. She seemed really nice and would be the one to come and sit with me at lunch and hang out with me at recess. She looked to have gone through most of her awkward puberty phase before I arrived at the school — her fully developed boobs were hard to miss.

I don't remember the chain of events, but a few months into the school year, two other girls in class started telling me that Shana wasn't as cool as I thought she was, and she was talking shit about me. It's amazing how today I can't remember what she said — shows you how unimportant those details are. At the time though, they consumed every waking thought.

The next thing I knew, I got a word-of-mouth invitation (an invitation I'd rather skip out on) from some other girls. "Shana wants to fight you at three o'clock on the playground pavement."

I felt sick to my stomach all day. *I don't know how to fight. What if she kills me? How do I even punch someone?* I just wanted to go home, but the other girls egged me on. "You're not going to let her talk shit about you — you have to show her that she can't mess with you. You *have* to fight."

Okay. Well, I had to prove my coolness, now I had to prove my worthiness and toughness too.

The end-of-day bell rang and as I grabbed my backpack and headed to the bus, I hoped (and prayed) she wouldn't be waiting for me, and I could get on the bus, go home, and pretend this never happened.

I was hopeful as I walked out of the school and tried to ignore my classmates following me, excited from the buzz. Word spreads quickly when there's a fight happening — especially when it's a girl fight.

Shit. There she was. What happened next was a blur. I

remember her hitting me with her palms (someone warned me she was a black belt, but I'm not sure I believe it). I don't remember how we stopped. It wasn't from being bloody and beaten. It was like we both had to put on a WWE show for our fellow classmates to prove something.

Whatever we were trying to prove, it didn't work. I don't even remember if one of us was declared a "winner." The next wave of fear I felt was sitting in the office while the principal called my mom at home. Somehow this all happened so fast that I still made it on the bus and got home in time. The only fear was what would happen when my dad came home from work. My mom wasn't so scary. She mostly yelled a lot, but my dad was louder — we sometimes called him the angry old Portuguese man.

I explained what happened. It was a non-fight. It was so far from any of the real fights I'd witnessed. I was grounded, but the principal waived the suspension. I probably would have been grounded much longer if the school suspension stuck.

The most awkward part of the whole thing? When my mom made me call and apologize to Shana. Looking back, I realize how Canadian of me this was.

My goal for the rest of the year was to survive. I didn't get in another fight. I'm sure there was some drama, but I did my best to remain cordial and keep everyone at arm's length. It was safer that way. I only had to go to that school for a year — good thing because I don't know how long I could keep up the dance of showing up exactly as everyone expected me.

My saving grace was that I'd do eighth grade in a brand-new school that had opened within a ten-minute walk of our new home.

I was about to go to my third school in three years — which sounds crazy, but I'd later (unintentionally) do this to my kids, so I now know that this is a good thing. This third change in schools for me was also a group change. We were all in this one together — we were *all* new kids.

Eighth grade felt powerful and fun. We were the big fishes in a little pond. Most of the kids were new and didn't know one another. We all had that in common. With it being a new neighborhood, everyone was new. Without there being that unspoken camaraderie and history, we all had a fighting chance to be cool.

The whole year continued to be an amazing one. I finally felt like one of the popular kids. I even had a boyfriend for the first time. At thirteen, that meant that we'd slow dance to Meat Loaf's "I'd Do Anything for Love" at the co-ed birthday parties in friends' basements. For the first time in a long time, life felt easy.

I'm leaving

Transitioning to high school was also an awkward time. A bunch of Catholic elementary school students coming together to wear uniforms for the first time in high school. There were still many ways to show coolness in a uniform — like how many pins you had on your tartan kilt. One pin, you were a loser; four, a slut; and two, you couldn't afford a third. Three was the magic number. Girls would make fun of you if your skirt was too long, but if it was too short (shorter than your fingertips while standing up), the vice principal would send you home to change.

Only one girl threatened to kick my ass that year. And I was legit afraid of her. She was a foot taller than me — I was done growing at five eight, and she *still* towered over me. Everyone knew she was a little crazy, so they stayed away from her. I full-on ignored her, and eventually she grew bored and stopped.

I don't know if I ever really found my groove in high school, but there were definitely fits and spurts of feeling like I belonged and then wanting to sit in the corner of the cafeteria and eat french fries (which I still did a lot anyway).

At home though, things started to get challenging.

When I was old enough to know what a healthy marriage looked like, I realized that what my parents had was definitely not it. Before my teenage years, I remember lots of fun and play at home. Home always felt safe, and I'm grateful my mom and dad created a loving home for my sister and I to grow up in. But later, when I was fifteen, I noticed that they fought — a lot. Mostly about money and chores and not wanting to do the same things or go to the same places.

There was a period where my dad worked a lot. His job as an auto shop manager for a large Canadian retail chain was an hour away, and most nights he'd get home after my mom, sister, and I had eaten dinner. He would eat alone and then maybe do some chores, bottle some homemade beer or wine, cut the grass, pour a few glasses of wine, and call it a day.

Even though I was a teenager, I felt like I could tell my dad most things. I always looked up to his charismatic ways, so his lack of presence didn't necessarily bother me until he moved out.

After what I can only recall as months of my dad coming home late, followed by screaming matches during which I'd lock myself in my purple bedroom with black-and-white Guess ads lining the walls, and wishing with all of my heart they'd get a divorce, it finally seemed I was going to have my wish.

My mom told my sister and me one day that my dad was moving out. I didn't have any details on where he was going, for how long, or why. All we knew was that he'd be leaving and living somewhere else. I had so many questions. *Why would he move out? Where would he go? What was wrong with us?*

We didn't know he was having an affair until my mom accessed his voicemail one day to discover *another* woman left him a voice message. It wasn't anyone we knew.

We didn't have a set schedule for seeing him, but he did come around often enough that I never considered him a deadbeat. I was angry and confused. I felt like *I* was the one who was betrayed.

"How could you do that to us?" I remember scream-crying from the top of the stairs one evening that he had been home. I've never been able to yell at anyone without crying at the same time — maybe why you'll rarely catch me yelling, especially in public. It's so much safer this way. The screaming-crying thing seems to frighten most people, and I'm certainly not proud of it. It also is quite confusing for the person on the receiving end who doesn't know if they should rub my arm or yell back.

I'd make my dad feel guilty for leaving and usually would take advantage of the situation and ask for money. He'd always give it to me. Being fifteen, I had my own teenage stuff to deal with. Crushes, hormones, playing on the volleyball team, maintaining straight As at school, and eventually picking up some habits like smoking and drinking the occasional beer at parties.

During the day, I'd get lost in thought during class, wondering how a divorce would look for my parents. Then in the evenings, I'd either travel to my first job as a cashier at a big retail store or head to parties on the weekend where I'd drink maybe two Molson Canadians; smoke a few du Mauriers or a Rothmans if I was desperate; be the first to leave, sensing the boringness of it all; and call it a night.

I wasn't really worried about getting caught. I mean, I wasn't getting drunk — I liked being in control far too much for that to happen. My mom and dad were wrapped up in their own stuff. I didn't even really enjoy smoking and drinking. I thought beer was disgusting, and very rarely was it actually cold since my friends usually snuck it around in their backpacks. I'd only smoke cigarettes in the evenings and felt a buzzy kind of disgustingness to the whole thing. Except that I was blending in. It felt comfortable and easy to do the things everyone else was doing. Some of my friends were getting into drugs — I remember smoking pot a few times, coughing like a maniac, and it making me just want to find a quiet spot and go to sleep. I wondered about the appeal. Weed is definitely not for the already unfussy.

I don't remember exactly how long my dad was gone — only a few months maybe. One Mother's Day, we woke up, and he was home, and home to stay.

My mom said it was the greatest Mother's Day gift ever. I

wasn't so sure. They didn't actually *fix* anything. He left for a while and merely came back — this all seemed way too straightforward. *This isn't going to work,* I thought to myself.

After that experience, he stayed, and things were definitely calmer and quieter, but they still weren't the poster family for how to do a happy and healthy marriage.

I always had a sneaking feeling that they didn't honestly want to be together, but they were waiting for something. I couldn't pinpoint what that *something* was — Jen and I to move out, maybe? As a teenager, who had a few casual, short-term boyfriends, I was no relationship expert, but I still had the insight that something was off. They appeared to be going through the motions, and I think my mom was terrified of taking the step of leaving her secure and familiar environment.

Early in my twenties, their twenty-fifth wedding anniversary was approaching, and my mom wanted a party. And by wanting a party, I mean it was more of a direct request to Jen and me. "Here's what I want to do for our anniversary." It felt like such ridiculousness, throwing an anniversary party for people who didn't seem to want to be married. Jen and I knew this but went through with it anyway. We were putting on a show. We knew that things weren't great, but here we were acting as if we're celebrating. What exactly are we celebrating anyway?

The party was uneventful. Thirty or so of our closest family and friends came to the house that Sunday afternoon in July to consume shrimp rings and burgers and brats off the grill, yell "Happy Anniversary," and eat vanilla cake with vanilla icing. It was so very weird.

The learning here — stay in a bad relationship, because change is harder than ending something that sucks. Stick it out — for the kids, for the image, for protecting your lifestyle and the status quo.

Less than a year into becoming a newlywed myself, my mom announced she was leaving my dad. She met someone else online, and was, ahem, engaged to marry him. This was all before the ink even touched their divorce papers.

Of course, I wasn't shocked at all. I had known since I was old enough to know what a healthy relationship looked like. Now, I was a statistic. My parents were divorced, and my mom remarried — the very same month their divorce was final.

I couldn't help but wonder — both of my parents had an affair, so what kind of message am I getting, even unconsciously about what happens in marriage? Is it that all marriages end with a cheating spouse? Is it that all people who say, "I do" will say "screw this" and cheat at some point?

Whatever the lesson, it didn't serve me in my early days of marriage. From day one, I operated on high affair-alert. Simply waiting for it to happen. If you peeked into our newlywed days, you wouldn't have seen lots of lovey-dovey stuff. You would have seen me, suspicious about everything, freaking out over every little thing, and plenty of fighting.

Ryan's parents are divorced too. We were statistically doomed to call it quits, and I was searching for a reason to as soon as I said *I do*. (When both sets of parents are divorced, the stats say that spouses are somewhere between 69 and 189 percent more likely to get divorced themselves, than are spouses with parents who have intact marriages.)

I'm happy to say that this phase passed quickly as this is no way to live. I had conversations with my parents around their relationship, their affairs, and their divorce, and made peace with it. I'm sixteen years into my own marriage and am happy to tell you we're beating all the odds.

II. CHOOSING CHANGE IN MY TWENTIES

"You cannot control the behavior of others, but you can always choose how you respond to it."

Roy T. Bennett

Oh, the twenties. In childhood it seems so much change happens to us. We barely even get to choose our underwear. When we hit adulthood, the choices in the buffet of life are limitless. We can vote, drink, date, go to college, get jobs. Suddenly, here I am: choosing change. Choosing to stay the same. We worry our decision will affect us for life — and it will. Sometimes we'll need to stop dicking around and pick — A or B, what'll it be?

I want to be rich and famous, but only if it's easy

When I was a kid, you would have seen me surrounded by piles of sketches and magazine photos taped to my walls and called me creative. You might have found me with a sketchpad in hand, drawing pictures of my cat, or coloring life-sized murals on my walls — true story, *and* I had my parents' permission. How cool is that? *Thanks, Mom and Dad!*

When I was ten, if you asked me what I wanted to be when I grew up, I would have told you my greatest wish was to become a rich and famous fashion designer and live in Paris. I had oodles of spiral-bound sketchbooks overflowing with original designs. Some were radical — things you'd only see in *Vogue,* and some were slight improvements of the clothes I was already wearing. You know, a high-fashion, Kmart-shopping ten-year-old.

Slowly, over the years, the dream of ruling the fashion world faded away, and I told myself a story — "Fashion school is too hard to get into, besides I don't have the money or know-how to sew," and, "I don't have any fashion sense."

When you grow up in a world of "be whatever you want," and then you spend your preteen years obsessing over your future career and fulfilling adults' incessant need to know "what do you want to be when you grow up?", you can get stuck at the very beginning, as soon as you actually start plotting how to take action, before you even take a step.

And that is how dreams come to a screeching stop.

All it took was for someone, and I can't even recall who, to ask me if I could sew. From that innocent little question, I realized I didn't know how to do something, so I just stopped. I didn't research fashion schools, didn't meet with a single designer, and concocted this whole story about how fashion was too hard.

What is up with that? I could do hard things.

Though I'd never admit it. Through most of my life I never really had to try all that hard — like with an all-my-guts kind of try. I gave my schoolwork a "pretty good" effort, got straight As, and received plenty of adoration and accolades. School was easy for me. I didn't really study, and it rarely felt "challenging." But as soon as I encountered something I thought might be difficult, I balked, didn't ask for help, and chose the next easy step.

Instead, I went to business school and studied marketing. Sure, there were creative components, but it wasn't full of color, creativity, and art — what I thought I'd be doing.

In school, I found my routines. Park in the same spot near the exit so I could minimize my time in traffic and order the same coffee. (Tim Hortons double-double — a reference only Canadians will understand. My snobby Starbucks tastes would shun it now.)

I had my rotations of different bars to hit each night of the week too.

Sunday was Finnegans.

Monday was Monaghan's, for twenty-five-cent wings.

Tuesday was Philthy McNasty's.

Wednesday was Emma's Back Porch.

Thursday was karaoke night (where I only sang once because I'm tone-deaf).

Saturday was Big Bucks.

From the looks of this list, it sounds like I spent lots of time in dive bars. But really, I grew up in one of the wealthiest towns in Canada. And we were not wealthy. Yes, I had everything I needed, but my parents favored spending beyond their means — a habit that's taken me forty years to break.

I was also the type-A student who did all my homework on time, never skipped class, and only went to the bar after I did my schoolwork. During most of my college days, I also worked full-time hours, clocking forty hours most weeks. I'm glad I took advantage of all that energy in my twenties because just writing this is making me tired.

And yes, I had friends. Not a lot, but I had a core group of people I could count on to come with me to all those bars every night of the week. On the odd occasion, I could go there alone and trust I'd run into some acquaintances.

Quite frequently, I was the designated driver. I'd have a drink or two and would force all my friends whose sorry asses I was hauling around to leave well before the last call. Sometimes they complained, but I'd tell them that if they wanted a ride, this Honda Prelude was leaving. (A car, by the way, which costs almost as much as my grown-up leased car — and I was twenty. I also left college debt-free, so I must have done something right.)

People in their twenties are screwed — we were (and still are) bombarded with the idea that we have endless choices, but we have to do what's "right," "easy," or "makes sense." All these contradictory messages are enough to make our heads spin.

I can't help but wonder what might have happened if I'd pushed myself to apply for fashion school. The threat of potential rejection was so strong that I didn't even try. If I didn't try, I could keep that dream inside the boundaries of my mind where it was safe. Safe from what exactly, I'm not sure. Safe from failure, safe from criticism, safe from success in my Parisian high-fashion dream life? Was this very prominent moment of playing it safe a look into the crystal ball of change and playing small?

Facing the choice of a career path, how did I decide that the more certain path was the best path, and the less certain one was the one to walk around at all costs? I spent my twenties walking slowly, staying within the boundaries, embracing responsibility — and choosing the safe road every time.

It's not you, it's me

Most of the moments that I'm the least proud of in my life were from my years of dating. I had to really excavate the back recesses of my mind to uncover these stories, and you probably won't hear me telling them to the kids at dinnertime. These dating years didn't stand out in my mind for being the good old days — at all.

Most of the guys I dated were fine, and then I had a string of bad boyfriends, ones who were either clingy, loser-y, untrustworthy, or just plain weird — and there was the one guy who cheated on me.

My very first "date" was in the eighth grade, and I'm not even sure it was a date at all. I certainly wasn't technically "allowed" to date until I was sixteen, so at thirteen, "dates" consisted of meeting my boyfriend at a friend's house party so we could slow dance, breathing on each other's necks for eight minutes and fifty-nine seconds, swaying to "November Rain." And maybe go in for some tonsil hockey before the song changed to Ace of Base's song "The Sign," and my girlfriends and I would bust out some synchronized choreography.

When a dude was starting to bore me, I hated having to be the one to hurt his feelings. I'd fall into the comfort trap almost every time. It felt so much easier to go with more of the same than to shake things up. When I was emotionally over them, I always secretly wished they'd break up with me, so I didn't have to initiate a difficult conversation. And sometimes I'd mentally check out, and passively sabotage the relationship until they'd stop calling or I finally summoned the courage to have the uncomfortable talk and tell the dude, "Sorry, it's not working anymore. It's not you, it's me."

This is embarrassing to admit, but I didn't really date in high school until my senior year, and it's not because I didn't want to. The guys I had crushes on didn't know I existed.

I also didn't get why you'd even *want* to date someone in your school. You'd have to see them every day and everyone talked about you. And if you were in the same class as each other — gross! What a distraction. I had straight As to maintain.

Instead, I actively pursued love interests from other schools, and a few older guys. Looking back — if that was *my* daughter, there would have been some bigger boundaries and maybe a lock on the *outside* of the bedroom door.

My first long-term relationship, in the twelfth grade, was with a guy who had graduated a year earlier and had a real job. So he'd be able to take me to the movies, pay for McDonald's, and supersize our fries so we could get more chances to win more junk at McDonald's Monopoly. We did all the stupid-ass shit like celebrate every damn month's anniversary. Happy two months! Here's a keychain I had engraved for you at the mall. We stuck it out for two-ish years, broke up a few times in there, and then I knew it was time to move on.

After that I went on a dating spree. I wasn't looking for a relationship — this is the way I'm going to word this story because my kids will read this book someday, and I don't want them thinking their mom was a ho.

Kids, when you read this, please know that mommy only had sex three times. Once for each of you, and once for the miscarriage that happened in between.

Now that that's out of the way, I liked changes of scenery when it came to dating. But then I'd take new dates to the same familiar places because I was too lazy to think of somewhere new to take people. Way too much work.

The nice guys bored me to tears. One guy even baked me cookies, and I dumped him because I "wasn't ready" — what in the actual fuck?

Dating called for constant (often exhausting) change that could actually sometimes be the easiest, safest thing because it didn't require me to choose or commit. When it gets hard, boring, or otherwise, you can quit and find a new one.

It wasn't until I met Ryan that I really started to embrace change and choose the more exciting fork in the road. And I learned I could date someone that was fun, smart, good-looking, and a good human. Imagine that.

Finding love in a dive bar

My parents asked me to visit Treasure Island, Florida — with them and my younger sister — our usual spot for the past fifteen years. I was twenty-two, which was pretty much too old to go on family vacations and at a phase in my life when I was trying very hard to be wild and crazy (I had to make up for all that time I'd lost proving my responsibility).

Well, it was a free vacation, so I said yes.

Usually, at dinner, my dad and I would enjoy some wine, leaving my mom to drive us back to our beach hotel. Once back at the hotel, my mom and sister would occasionally come with us for a drink at a nearby bar if there was a live band playing.

You could count on them to duck out early, though, and leave my dad and me to close the place.

On this particular evening, it was after midnight, and my dad and I were taking our final sips of our Corona Lights at Ricky T's beach bar. We decided we'd check out the bar next door, the VIP Lounge — a Mexican restaurant and dive-ish bar (though it's much nicer today).

While we were at Ricky T's, I noticed a group of guys around my age walk into the VIP Lounge. This was a tourist spot, so there were lots of people around. Since I was with my dad I wasn't exactly in "pick-up mode" — I noticed them and felt a sudden desire to be alone or with girlfriends — basically anyone but my dad.

I mostly noticed the guy with the tattoos. He appeared to be a little older than the other guys, and I made the judgment that he must be a loser for hanging out with dudes younger than him. Soft gray T-shirt, jeans, flip-flops, dark-rimmed glasses — sturdy, handsome. He didn't look like my usual "type." I never paid any attention to dudes under six feet tall and certainly not the ones covered in ink.

My dad suggested I go into the VIP Lounge and grab a seat while he signed the bill for our Coronas and peed.

I walked into the VIP, which had a lot of flashy neon and brass. It was thick with smoke (in the early 2000s you could still smoke in lots of bars) and full of people slinging back shots. The wall behind the bar was lined with photos of what looked to be the VIP's favorite (drunk and happy) customers.

I sat next to the dude with the dark-rimmed glasses and tattoos stretching all the way down to his forearm. I may have muttered, "Hi" — I really don't remember — and we exchanged names.

"I'm Ryan."

He didn't look like a Ryan. I hoped I could remember his name. To remember a name, I need to recite it over and over in my head to help it sink in. We didn't strike up a conversation right away, but he was smoking Marlboro menthols — my favorite at the time, especially because Marlboros weren't available north of the border. What's a girl to do? I poked fun at him for smoking menthols and asked him for one.

After lighting my smoke, and puffing the minty tobacco above my head, the tattoo-dude told me he was from New York, and he worked at this place called Bloomberg. I didn't admit it to him at the time, but I didn't know what Bloomberg was. I was a recent marketing grad and working for a major Canadian retailer.

My mind turned to fantasy, and I imagined him swaggering through the streets of New York City in a navy three-piece suit, tie, his signature dark-rimmed glasses, and looking oh-so-suave. Thinking about the dark-rimmed glasses and crisp, dark suit concealing the tattoos and smoking habit was pretty hot.

We chatted about our work, what we loved about it, and he thought it was cool that I was Canadian. He thought Canadians were ethnic and somehow exotic — hilarious.

My dad joined us after settling up at the other bar and grabbed a barstool to my right; Ryan to my left. My dad and I would exchange some comments here and there, but we weren't overly engaged in any kind of deep and lively conversation.

After we were married, Ryan told me that he thought I was a hooker (a *hooker*, can you believe it?) and my dad was a customer. I wish I were kidding.

Now, remember I was on a family vacation. I was wearing a knee-length jean skirt and a white V-neck tank top with plenty of coverage. Hardly inappropriate. Because he noticed my dad and I at the other bar, saw me alone in the VIP, then this older man rejoined me at the VIP, and we barely spoke, he thought this old man was an unwelcome (but paying) guest.

He told me that he was about to tell my dad to piss off and leave me alone when I stopped mid-conversation, realizing I hadn't introduced them, and said, "Oh, Ryan, meet my dad, Tony."

They shook hands and proceeded to converse more than the tattooed glasses guy and I did. I was a little tipsy at the time, and so was my dad. Okay, I was *drunk*. I definitely wasn't looking at this as a pick-up situation.

The three of us enjoyed lively conversation until the lights came on in the bar, blinding everyone — a blatant call to get out of there. I learned that the tattoo guy was entertaining some of his mothers' friends' kids and took them out as a favor.

He was sober as he was their designated driver for the night. His mom lived in Florida, and he was visiting her for Mother's Day. *How sweet,* I thought, forgetting all previous loser-y judgments.

When we were ready to part ways, I told him there was a good bar around the corner that has live music and I'd be there tomorrow night. I suggested he join us, and he agreed. We stood up to leave. *Holy shit, he's shorter than me.* I was wearing flip-flops that had a smidge of a platform.

Well, I guess we're done.

At that time, I had a thing about shorter guys. My McDreamy was tall, dark, and handsome — not short, thick, and needing SPF 90.

I'd never been to New York City, and he offered to show me around if I ever decided to visit. He gave me a business card, and I wrote my number drunkenly with lipstick on the back of another one while my dad sat drunk on the curb outside the bar and waited for us to make our exchange.

The next day, I realized that I really did drink too much the night before; I was sick most of the morning. Oh, to be twenty-two.

Early in the afternoon, though, I got a phone call from him. He said he was at the beach with his mom, and he was looking at a hotel that was a few doors down from where we were staying.

"Oh, cool," I said. I was not registering that he was there to *see me.* Stupid, stupid, stupid! I was feeling super crappy and hungover, so I didn't even entertain the idea of going to the beach.

I thought he was calling to chat about meeting at the bar later to listen to the band. I told him roughly when I'd be there, and I'd see him later. He said he'd try to make it. I was leaving to go home the next day.

That night, my mom, dad, sister, and I were at the bar listening to live music. My mom wanted to see this short dude with the tattoos and glasses. I kept watching the door for a sign of him but didn't see him. He was a no show.

Oh well — he was too short for me anyway.

The next day we headed home to Canada, and I didn't give the whole exchange much thought.

Meeting American strangers in the woods

Two weeks later, I was sitting at work, a little listless, when I felt the urge to send tattoo dude an email. I jokingly gave him crap for not coming out to the bar to meet me that night and told him if he was ever in Toronto, to come and say hi.

I was completely surprised when I received an email back from him — like twenty minutes later. In his email, he told me he'd intended to meet me but had fallen asleep at his mom's around 10:00 p.m. that night, and by the time he woke up the next morning I would have already been gone. He also admitted the awkwardness of coming out alone to join my whole family and me at a bar. He didn't yet know just how friendly Canadians are.

He also told me he was about to send me an email but got mine first. Was he lying? Maybe, I'll never know. It doesn't matter. We quickly fell into a habit of emailing back and forth all day long while we sat at our respective offices in Manhattan and Toronto. I'd get home from work and head straight to MSN Messenger and we'd chat until bedtime.

We'd text during our respective train commutes into our respective cities. We spent the better portion of our day communicating electronically. I loved it when I'd see a new email pop up from him. Sometimes we'd have multiple email threads going on — my favorite!

One night he asked, "Would a phone call be out of the question?" Ack! This was real now; he wanted to *talk* to me? On the phone? What were we going to talk about? Oh, this was going to be totally awkward.

He called me and our landline (remember those?) gave the special ring that meant the call was coming from a long-distance number outside of Canada. Flutters.

We were chatting. We were flirting.

A few days later, after I'd spent the night at a girlfriend's house, Ryan and I were chatting on MSN Messenger while the rest of the girls were lounging and nursing hangovers from one-dollar drinks. I told him I'd forgotten what he looked like — I met him once, only for a few hours, in a dark bar, and did I mention I was tipsy? He sent me a black-and-white photo.

I showed my girlfriends the image on the computer screen — "What do you think?" The consensus was positive — he was a winner. Then I read his latest message, "My family has a cabin in the Adirondacks — I think it's halfway in between us, maybe we could meet there?"

I turned to the girls, "He wants to meet at his cabin in New York! Should I go?" They freaked. "You're nuts," "You don't know him," and "What if he's a crazy psycho killer?"

Then someone said, "Do it."

"I'm doing it," I said, as I quickly typed back to him, "Sure!" It felt so very 'Meg Ryan, *You've Got Mail*' of me.

I couldn't get the trip out of my mind for the rest of the day — or the next week.

Before the trip, I told my dad, "Remember that guy we met in the bar in Florida? Well, I'm going to his cabin in New York."

I don't recall my dad asking many questions. If that was one of my kids, I'd have hidden the car keys.

In the days leading up to the trip, Ryan told me all the things we'd do there. Totally clean, fun things — we'd go to the beach, do some hiking or boating, eat ice cream by the lake, enjoy the cottage town, then drink too many apple martinis by the campfire. Appletinis were totally our signature drink back then — they paired well with the Marlboro menthols.

I packed up my Honda with some cottage essentials (gummy bears, Diet Coke, and salt-and-vinegar chips), stopped at the mall for some thinner-soled flip-flops so I wouldn't tower over him, left work early, and hit the road toward the Buffalo border.

"Where are you going?" the US border patrol guard asked me.

"Old Forge," I responded.

"Where's that?" he probed.

"I have no idea." My honest answer. Not wanting to sound like an idiot, I waved my map printout in the air and said, "But it looks like it's about four hours from here."

I'm surprised they let me through with that lame response.

We texted along the way, coordinating our arrival times. The plan was to meet in an Old Navy parking lot off I-90, in Utica.

You might be wondering if I was freaking out.

Yes, majorly — the whole ride there. Sunroof open on a hot June afternoon, as I munched gummy bears and sipped Diet Coke, I panicked and thought about turning around at least three dozen times.

This is nuts, what if he's a psycho?
What if he's ugly?
What if he thinks I'm ugly?
What if we have nothing to talk about?
What if he's boring?
What if he's going to bring me out to the woods to kill me?

As planned, we met in the Old Navy parking lot — he arrived first. I got there and found him waiting in his car. *Shit — do I hug him?* I mean, we'd flirted for like a month and spent a hundred hours texting more smiley faces than a twelve-year-old girl. We hugged, and after being in the car for so long, we both had to use the bathroom, so we ran into the Old Navy.

Holy awkward, Batman.

We were in the flesh now. No more screens to hide behind. Person-to-person — just us. We still had another hour to go to get to the cabin. He had directions; I was to follow him.

I drove behind him, continuing my freak-out and running all kinds of scary scenarios through my head. If I turned around really quickly, maybe he wouldn't notice, then I'd just ignore his calls until he stopped calling.

We arrived at the cabin, and it was cute — very rustic — the kind with the toilet *outside*. Not the kind of cabin I was used to — but I didn't quite know what to expect anyway. He had to hook something up outside to get water or gas or something; I have no fucking clue. I just stood there watching in case I could be useful. I might have held the flashlight for him.

Then I saw it.

He bent over, and the handle of a handgun peeked out from the waistband of his jeans. The first thought that popped into my head — run! Get in the car, don't say a word, and drive like hell.

Canadians don't have guns. Canadian border patrol agents didn't even start carrying until 2005. I was twenty-two, naïve, and totally ignorant about firearm "etiquette."

Finally, I choked out, "What is that?" Obviously, I knew what it was, but I wanted to make sure he knew I saw it.

Ryan said plainly, "A pistol — I'm in the woods." As if it was a totally rational explanation.

"Oh, okay," I answered, sarcastically, not understanding why you'd need a gun for protection in the woods. "Can you leave that thing in the car until we leave?" I asked. It seemed like a perfectly reasonable expectation.

"What good will it do in the car?" he argued.

I wasn't fucking around with this American psycho killer. "Just do it."

He obliged, and we went out to dinner and drank too many appletinis that night.

The next morning, I emerged from the room to see something that made me think I must still be dreaming.

There was a deer with its front hooves in the entryway of the cabin. With one hand, Ryan was feeding gummy bears to the deer. With the other, he was holding a pistol to the deer's head.

Yep.

"What are you doing?" I asked quietly, but with a hint of *what the fuck*, not wanting to startle either of them in this fragile moment.

Without hesitation, he said, "In case he bucks."

This was marriage material.

I knew there was something about this guy, something different. And not just the tattoos or the glasses or the way he wielded a pistol at Bambi's head (sarcasm).

That first weekend was amazing. I didn't want it to end. I didn't want to leave.

As the weekend drew to a close, we headed south toward Utica and took our turns down I-90 to travel our separate ways.

Ryan, eastbound, toward Albany.

Me, westbound, toward Buffalo.

By the time I returned home, we had plans for our next meeting, and the meeting after that, and another one a few weeks out — just in case.

Until that one trip to Toronto that involved three very special love notes and changed everything.

I wrote you something

Ryan and I spent the next four months after our first "date" in the Adirondacks hopping on planes and driving between Poughkeepsie, New York, and Oakville, Ontario. It was October now, and Ryan was flying up for a weekend rendezvous.

He'd been acting super weird, asking me over and over again in the weeks leading up to this trip how much I loved him.

"But *why* do you love me?" he'd probe.

Ugh, why does he keep asking me this? He's so annoying. Is he that insecure? Is dating this guy going to be all about me proving my feelings to him? How incredibly annoying.

The night before he was scheduled to fly to Toronto, he was totally MIA. And these were the days of flip phones. My text messages were going unanswered, and he wasn't calling me back. When he finally did return my call, it was late, and he said something about having been at Duane Reade, which we don't have in Canada. "What the fuck is Duane Reade?" I asked.

Something about it being a magical place where you could buy pain meds and wine — and all under the same roof. A foreign concept to me in Canada.

Something was up, and I had a sneaking suspicion he might be proposing. We were dating long distance, and even though it had only been four months since our first date, we were having conversations about who might move where. Except when there's a border in between your man and you, it's not so simple.

The inconveniences of our international relationship forced us to make a bigger choice more quickly. We got pretty serious pretty fast. These thoughts were going down just five months after those first Coronas and Marlboros.

In case you were wondering, I couldn't just pick up and decide to move to the US — the immigration enforcement agency frowns on that behavior. I was about to learn just how much.

Preparing for our weekend together, I had booked us a hotel room in downtown Toronto, in the busy and hip Yonge and Queen area. I would pick him up from the airport, then we would catch up while wandering around the city and enjoying good food.

I planned to leave work a few hours before his flight arrived, check in to the hotel, and leave a little surprise for him in our room. That surprise was a hundred or so small sticky notes (don't tell my old boss), each one with a hand-scribbled note giving a reason why I loved him. Maybe this would be enough reassurance for him that I wasn't messing around. It was a bold move, a big gesture, and definitely out of my comfort zone.

I checked into the hotel, navigated my way to room 511, and plastered the little yellow love notes all over the room. On light switches, the floor, lamps, phone, mirrors, tables, and desk — I might have even put one on the toilet.

Making a big gesture like this made my heart flutter with what I think was excitement. Then I started getting cold feet. I'd never done anything like this before. I was feeling exposed. *What if he thinks it's stupid? What if he laughs? What if he thinks it's too much, too soon?*

Oh well, it was done now. I sure as hell wasn't going to clean up all those notes. It was time to head to the airport anyway. As I left the room, I looked around, feeling like hot shit. I smiled, turned the lights off, quickly walked down to the parking garage for my electric-blue Prelude, and zipped off to YYZ.

A scene that always makes my eyes well up is watching couples reunite at the airport. These are the people looking like they're ready to explode, carrying flowers or balloons and watching the gate doors intensely for their person to appear.

Ryan came through the door, looking exhausted and a little distracted but excited to see me. He wrapped me up in his substantial arms with the best bear hug. With my American boy on my arm, we headed back to the hotel to drop off his bags and grab dinner.

I was excited for the weekend. Our weekends together were always carefree and mostly agenda-free. We tried to soak up as much joy from each other as we could before we parted ways for another few weeks.

We arrived back at the hotel room. I stuck the plastic hotel key into the slot and held my breath as I waited for that satisfying click of the door unlocking and the flash of the little green indicator. For some reason, I always feel like I'm getting away with something during that exact moment.

This time was even bigger, remember — I was hot-shit, sticky note–writing McGee.

I walked into the room first, Ryan trailing me. I flipped the lights on as he dropped his bag.

Eyes darting around the room, I was stunned. Frantic. My heart sank.

Walking around the suite in utter disbelief, I realized the notes were gone! All that writing, the anticipation for his reaction, the thought of him collecting and reading each note, one by one.

All that love. All that writing. Shat on.

I couldn't help it — I started to cry.

Imagine you were Ryan at this point. He was totally like, "What in the actual hell is wrong with this chick?"

I didn't want to tell him why I was upset, but I couldn't just keep crying without offering up some explanation. I'm also the worst liar in the world, so making something up was out of the question.

I spilled it. I spoke through the discomfort and told him about the notes, what I wrote, detailing my suspense and excitement. My description, of course, could never match the actual thing. We deduced housekeeping must have turned the room down and left with my notes in a garbage bag.

Disappointed but determined not to let an overachieving housekeeper ruin our night, we headed out for dinner. Ryan insisted we make a stop at the front desk first. He told the manager what happened while I stood there, completely embarrassed — yes, I'm the weirdo who wrote a bunch of sticky notes. He thanked them for "making his girlfriend cry." They apologized but couldn't really do anything. I mean, what would they do? Go dig through the hotel garbage bin? And then what? Show him all the notes in one big, messy, trash-splattered pile?

So we did what we did best back then — sipped apple martinis and munched on calamari and nachos. Eventually, after catching up, it was getting late, so we walked back to the hotel. Back in the sticky note–free room, I was still feeling a twinge of sadness. I got ready to climb into bed while Ryan was lingering in the other room of the suite. He was there a long time — like a really, really long time. *What the hell is he doing?*

After I'd asked him once or twice, he eventually showed up. Serious-faced and holding some small, white pieces of hotel stationery (which is a lame excuse for stationery). I asked what he was doing in an annoyed, worried, what-are-you-up-to, I'm-tired-and-need-sleep tone.

He finally spoke. "I wrote you some notes of my own."

Sweet! I *love* love letters. Having dated long distance, we filled in our constant text messaging, emails, and phone calls with random cards and letters. Way better than email.

He just stood there, holding them.

I asked, "Are you going to give them to me?"

He hesitated and stood still in the doorway between the bedroom and the hotel suite. "No."

I was annoyed. *Why the hell would you write me something then not give it to me? Don't waste my time with your silly games, I need to go to sleep.*

I tried to persuade him, unsuccessfully for a minute or two. He had a white-knuckled grip on those babies. *They must be good — or bad. Oh shit — what if he flew here to break up with me?*

I was about to say *fuck it* and go to sleep when he finally handed them over.

There were three pieces of hotel notepad paper with some words on them.

They read:

Note 1: I love you

Aww, feeling kinda melty and my right armpit is starting to sweat — a normal reaction for me.

Note 2: I want to spend the rest of my life with you

OH SHIT, is this the big moment? The one we dream of? Is he really proposing? OMG! OMG! OMG! OMGGGGGG!

Note 3: Will you marry me?

Dead.

By now, I was crying for the second time that night, with my hand over my mouth. Shakily, I looked up. He was now down on the proverbial bended knee and took out the goods (the ring!).

Holy shit! This is happening; this is real! That is a real ring! Is it for me?

I think I said the word "yes." The rest was a blur of squealing and crying and trying to get Ryan up off his knee to hug me. He asked, "Did you say yes? I think you did."

Um, "YES!"

After God knows how long, I looked at the ring that was too loose for my finger, but so perfect.

So simple. He didn't even ask what I wanted; he just picked it. Lucky for me, he's got better taste than I do.

I felt electric, tingly, and alive. We were getting married.

Four months and three days later, we stood in front of each other again — shakily, in part from celebrating with family and friends too much the night before — and said *I do* on Valentine's Day, 2004.

We said yes to change — changing our relationship status, living situation, daily routines — forever. The change on my end required me to change my address, including my country, and eventually my citizenship.

That's Miss Canada to you

Do you know those people who don't need to decide where they're going to live? Maybe you're one of them. These folks meet someone a town or two over and live within thirty miles of where they grew up. Easy, done, no decision fatigue there.

After deciding to get married, the next big decision Ryan and I needed to make was where to live — Canada or the US? We considered both, and it came down to this — I was fresh out of college and a year into my corporate job, whereas Ryan was a few years in and made more money than me. Alrighty then, I was immigrating to the US. I was excited to live in the land of opportunity.

Having grown up an hour from the US–Canada border, I'd spent a lot of time in the US as a kid. We had family in Michigan and vacationed there a few times a year. If you live in Southern Ontario, "going to the US" isn't all that big a deal.

Some of my Canadian friends and family called me a traitor, and I'd overhear comments at dinners like, "I'd never leave Canada, this is the greatest country on earth." I never confronted anyone when I heard these things. I've been in more debates than I can count about which is the "better" country.

And the answer I keep coming to — neither. Both countries have their positives and negatives. What usually comes up is health care. "But you get free health care!" Americans say. And yes, you don't take out your wallet to see a doctor in Canada, but you pay for it through higher taxes, lower wages, and higher cost of goods on all things — food being a big one. Having lived in both countries, I can say both health-care systems are far from perfect.

We explored a few paths to my US residency and decided that the fiancé(e) (K-1) visa made the most sense. With a fiancé visa, we got to do all kinds of fun things like proving our relationship to immigration with photos, flight receipts, and documentation of emails and phone calls. The thing about the fiancé visa is that you have no idea when it's going to go through.

So we kept making trips to see each other, wondering when our final interview would happen, and I'd finally get my visa to move to the US.

Traveling to the US from Canada when you're engaged to a US citizen and waiting for your papers to process is *not* for the faint of heart. Every time I crossed the border, I was often on the other end of extensive questioning. They also detained me a few times and searched my car. I never had anything to hide — I was just crossing the border to visit my fiancé. Which I later discovered is probably up there with announcing a trunk full of pot. I was still scared shitless every time I crossed that border patrol would somehow discover that I'd unknowingly broken some law.

One time I was flying from Buffalo to New York City to save six hours of driving for Halloween weekend and the wedding of one of Ryan's friends. I had what you'd expect a twenty-three-year-old to pack for a wedding and a Halloween weekend — a black strapless cocktail dress and a fun costume.

My costume that year — Miss Canada. I had a toque (that's Canadian for winter hat), a red plaid flannel shirt, and a sash I'd customized with red fabric paint to read "Miss Canada." Also, since we were getting married, I happened to have a few bridal magazines in the trunk of my car.

As a young, engaged person who followed everyone's rules, you'd think this would not be a problem.

That is until you try to cross a country's border and they tell you to pull over to the special section, where you get an extra search. The old lady at the booth gave zero shits that I had a flight to catch soon in Buffalo and wasn't going to make it to the airport on time.

As she combed through my suitcase with gloved hands, she pulled out the sash and with the most serious face, asked me accusingly, "What is *this*?"

Instinctively, I laughed. Then I realized she was serious. Wiping my smile away, I said, "Um, that's my Halloween costume." I tried explaining the whole concept of plaid, winter hats, and being Canadian to her, and she did not connect the dots, or even see the humor.

She paused a minute, huffed loudly, then told me, "I think you're lying, and *you're* the one getting married this weekend."

What in the actual fuck?

I'm following all your country's immigration rules. We applied, we paid thousands of dollars, and are doing it the right way. I'm waiting for my visa. I have a job, a leased car, and debts in Canada, and I am in no way getting married this weekend.

I asked her, baffled, "Do you really think I'd get married in this dress?" Pointing to my black strapless cocktail dress folded up in my suitcase. What fuckery.

From that point on, I made sure to travel with a letter from my boss stating that they expected me to return to work on Monday, plus copies of bank statements and my business cards to show I had ties to Canada and wasn't jumping the border for an illegal wedding.

I don't know exactly what I said, but they finally gave me my Halloween costume back, I made it to the airport right on time, went out for way too many Halloween drinks as Miss Canada, and went to Ryan's friends' wedding.

With all these forks in the road, it would have been so much easier to choose a nice, local boy to marry. One that didn't require all this extra work, time, money, and literal roadblocks just to spend a weekend together. And yet, when we were together, I knew there was no other choice I'd want to make.

The interview that would determine our fate

I received the letter we'd been waiting for from US Citizenship and Immigration Services about my fiancé visa interview. It was happening in a few weeks in Montreal — six hours from where I lived near Toronto. There were clear instructions on when and where to go. I didn't even need to bring Ryan with me. Well, he *wanted* to come; he thought it would further prove my case, so he arranged to join me.

Assuming that everything would go as planned at our interview, we'd travel to Montreal on Sunday, have our interview on Monday (hopefully get my fiancé visa), head back to my parents' house, drive the seven hours, cross the border declaring residency, then move into Ryan's place in Poughkeepsie on Tuesday. Then we'd get married on Saturday, which also happened to be Valentine's Day.

The next few weeks were a whirlwind of contingencies. We had too many "if this, then that" plans running through our minds to keep track of. Here's what we didn't know: if the fiancé visa would be approved, if setting a wedding date was a bad idea, when I could work, and when I could even get a New York state driver's license.

I'm part type A (I like clarity) and part unfussy (ah, we'll figure it out). Ryan definitely likes plans more than me. After our first rendezvous in the Adirondacks, he called me to schedule trips for all of June. With all the unknowns though, I was beginning to be a stress-bag. And who else to take it out on but my soon-to-be husband (though I could hardly utter those words at the time) and family?

Once we had the interview date, we banked on getting a stamp of immigration approval and went ahead with wedding plans, hoping for the best. Only a handful of our family and friends knew about the wedding, which was going to happen at a courthouse in Wappingers Falls, New York. Then we'd plan the big fancy wedding that everyone could attend later that year, probably September in Canada.

We traveled to Montreal by train that Sunday, checked into our hotel, and nervously made sure we had rehearsed answers to all the questions we anticipated. It was as if we were faking a relationship and were worried that they'd call us out. We had a legit relationship and really had nothing to worry about.

We were antsy with fear, thinking about what could happen if they denied my visa. What would we do? Could our relationship even survive an immigration delay? Could Ryan immigrate to Canada instead? What about our wedding plans?

Monday morning, we traveled to the US Embassy in Montreal, and the front desk person directed me to a room where the interviewer would join me behind plexiglass. They said that Ryan could come in but was supposed to keep quiet.

Well, our interviewer came in, grabbed my file folder, and flipped through a stack of photos Ryan had sent in with our application. She looked right over me and started asking Ryan questions about where he was from, and they talked about some nearby areas I knew nothing about.

The whole thing lasted all of five minutes. She said they'd call my name in the waiting room when it was ready, and my visa would be attached to my Canadian passport. *Well, that was easy! We did it!*

We took the six-hour train ride back to my parent's house, I packed up the rest of my things into Ryan's silver Dodge Dakota, and we headed out to my new country and new home Tuesday morning. I didn't have any long and drawn-out good-byes with my family — I'd see them three days later for the rehearsal and dinner, and the wedding on Saturday.

It was basically *see you later*. I didn't realize that my relaxed attitude toward moving away from home was misplaced until later when my dad called and told me that my mom cried the entire morning I left.

I had been so wrapped up in the excitement of my life and all these changes that I didn't pause to consider how my big transition to married life in another country affected anyone else.

The thing about big changes is that if you're whacked with them or whack a bunch of them yourself all at once or in close succession, they don't feel all that big and scary. One big change, if you have time to stew in the impact, can feel huge and heavy. But once you get into the momentum — huge change, big change, medium change, massive change — it all just becomes life and you roll with it.

Sometimes a microscopic change — something simple like adding a gym visit to your day or finding fifteen minutes to meditate — feels so dang hard. And yet a huge one can be like nothing. Quit your job, get married, move to a different country. The next minute, you're sipping a margarita, looking around and wondering how you got here — these people, this place, this house, this life.

Opening the floodgates for more expansive change

The wedding was a fun experience and nerve-wracking all at the same time.

It was Valentine's Day, and our vow exchange happened in a courthouse, with a judge — a family friend of Ryan's — performing the marriage. I wore a satiny white pantsuit with a silver top and silver heels; it was perfect for the occasion.

Awwwwww.

That's the sound people often make when I tell them Valentine's Day is our anniversary. It means a few things — first, it's almost impossible to forget our anniversary. Stores and ads remind us starting in January. And yet Ryan will still sometimes manage it. One year, he forgot that it was Valentine's Day. Which meant that he forgot it was our anniversary. I'm not that fussy wife who expects to be showered with roses — I'd much rather save that money for a nice dinner out or a trip — but a "Hey honey, I remembered" is nice.

The other thing that sucks about a Valentine's Day anniversary is going out to dinner to celebrate your anniversary means that everyone else is out there doing the same. People dress up and pay too much money for a fancy fixed menu when all I want to order is the seafood with linguine.

Back to the wedding day.

Here I was, twenty-three, in a new country, in front of my family and some of Ryan's, plus a few friends.

I don't remember a single thing from the ceremony, but at the end, once we exchanged rings, Ryan mouthed the words, "I love you," and all the emotions I had bottled up for the entire week leading up to that one moment spilled out into Niagara Falls–like tears.

I was feeling so many things that I couldn't pinpoint a single emotion. Excitement for a new life? Anticipation for marriage? It was all wrapped up together into the biggest single fucking change of my life so far — one that I had no idea at the time would kick off the next sixteen years (and counting) of incredible, mind-altering changes.

And it all started with a chance, late-night encounter at a Florida dive bar, then saying yes to traveling into the woods, and resisting the urge to turn around.

I lived with my parents through college (it's how I finished school without student loans) and led what some would call a pretty sheltered life. It wasn't until we celebrated our most recent wedding anniversary that I was finally able to grasp just how much that single, most prominent change set me on a path I couldn't have imagined.

Once I shoveled the last of the wedding cake into my face while sitting under a big blanket in my new home, I wondered if I had bitten off a larger piece of change-pie (or change-cake, in this case?) than I could chew. I ate the whole dang piece — who leaves cake on their plate?

New country.

New home.

New relationship.

New roommate.

New routines.

I have to grocery shop for two people now? How the hell do I cook chicken? This was when I discovered the Food Network and Rachael Ray.

New friends.

New family.

New car — which also happened to be a stick-shift pick-up truck. I learned how to drive it in upstate New York, in the winter. I panicked when I came to stoplights on a hill and was terrified of rolling backward and stalling. Which I did — a lot.

It was that, or I'd sit in the condo all day. I *had* to learn how to drive that truck. Learning how to master the stick shift was how I'd find freedom. Or I could audition for the next round of *Real Housewives of New York* with this glamorous life of mine.

New job — which was unpaid. Because of immigration rules, I didn't have a work permit yet. This is why we decided to get married right away after I moved to the US on my fiancé visa. With the K-1 visa, you have three months from the time you establish residency to get married. We got 'er done in four days so we could get the other paperwork going — green card application, work permit, and travel documents.

I couldn't work in or even leave the US at this point — and I had no idea when I'd be able to do so either. As someone who'd had a job since the age of fifteen and worked two jobs through college, turning off my ambition to become a housewife and be completely reliant on her new husband was not a change I embraced easily — at all.

I'd been dry-eyed when I drove away from Toronto the week before, but I cried my eyes out when my family left a few days after the wedding. I was alone. I was married, sure, but it was just me now. I had to navigate this whole thing by myself.

I wish I could say I did this gracefully. I didn't. I was a miserable bitch to live with. I questioned my decision to move, immigrate, and get married many times every day. I thought, *I should have just stayed in Canada in my parents' house where it was comfortable and familiar.*

And the second I had those thoughts, I also knew that wasn't the right answer either.

During those newlywed days, we fought — a lot. We didn't travel for a honeymoon on account of me not having a job and living on one income now. It didn't help at all that Ryan commuted over two hours each way to work in Manhattan. I'd drive him to the Poughkeepsie train station at 5:00 a.m., would sometimes go back home to bed and try to sleep some more, then get up and begin my day — alone. This is not what I imagined marriage to look and feel like. I missed our carefree, responsibility-free weekends together. Plucked from real life, the only thing we had to *do* was be present together.

Here I was, this ambitious corporate ladder-climber just waiting to be handed my next ladder. The days went on and on — cooking and cleaning and doing housewife things. So I did what any new housewife would do — took my Canadian credit cards and went shopping. I felt like I needed some kind of compensation for all this work. Ryan didn't know about this spending, and he probably would have been annoyed at the time — I buy candles and new flip-flops; he buys motorcycles and pets.

Looking for some more exciting things to fill my time, I got a gym membership and worked out twice a day — finally getting rid of those college beer pounds.

Ryan brought up the idea of getting a dog. A dog was a big deal to me. Ryan always had dogs growing up; me, we had cats. At least a dog was a more neutral commitment than marriage — I feed the dog, walk the dog, and pick up shit. He talked me into getting a rescue dog from a local animal shelter in Beacon. At least with a dog, I wouldn't feel so lonely, and I'd have something to do other than cobble together thirty-minute meals. I picked up my first dog, Snoopy (who we later renamed Wesley), one afternoon. He sat in the front seat of the truck the entire thirty-minute ride home, just staring at me with his soulful brown eyes. I nervously thought he was going to eat me. He was a pit bull mix. Because of discrimination against the breed, we had his vet records say "American Bulldog Mix";

otherwise, we'd never get into an apartment or boarding facility.

Having cats growing up, I had no freaking clue how to deal with a dog. *Do I have to pick up his shit with a bag? How does that work? With my hand?*

Wesley was a royal pain in the ass from the second he got home until his last smelly breath. He peed on the floor at least once a day in the beginning, shit under the kitchen table too many times to count, ate shoes, scared all the neighbors, and broke out of every single crate we bought him.

There was one time where he had to crap while crated and somehow managed to point his asshole at the wall so he'd keep his crate bed nice and clean. *Thanks for painting the walls for us, Wesley-roo!*

Even though he was high maintenance, I loved that dog. He was my best friend in those early days. When you have no friends, no job, and can't visit your hometown, you get a dog. That dog enjoyed walks five times a day. I trained him, and he only listened to me.

He was *my* dog. He was by my side every single day, and then when we had kids — Jacob, then Talia — he was their buddy too.

Even though my housewife days all felt the same, I was making little changes to catch up to the big changes I'd just made: learning how to cook chicken, leaving my family, using a new currency, getting used to the imperial measurement system, getting a dog, and learning to no longer say, "eh." Not that anyone told me to — I became extremely self-conscious of sounding like I didn't belong to the place where I wasn't sure I belonged.

These little changes cracked me open in a way that would make room for more expansive change. I went from my safe and familiar little bubble in my parents' house to shattering every comfort I knew. This gave me the ability to rebuild my life however I wanted.

III. RIDING THE CHAOS CRAZY TRAIN

"You may not control all the events that happen to you, but you can decide not to be reduced by them."

Maya Angelou

For a long time, I assumed most people had been through an absurd amount of changes. But after years of needing seven minutes to explain where I'm 'from' when I meet someone new at a party, I realize that maybe I've stacked up a lot of change in a short period of time. Here, I share how to make hard decisions, find clarity, have difficult conversations, create stability amidst change, and find the fun. And then, riding the chaos to find identity and strength after a mighty pileup of changes — sometimes, right in the messy middle.

Why am I puking so much?

Why am I so sick?

We were living in Chicago at that point (our third move, but more about that later). I had stopped obsessing over how to cook chicken after my US work permit came through, and I'd traded the Food Network for Facebook and fancy work clothes. During one of my corporate holiday parties, Ryan and I were out until way past last call dancing and drinking all the drinks. Definitely puffed a few cigarettes, too — I was still a social smoker back then.

I spent most of the next morning driving the white porcelain bus to yak-ville. Out of nowhere, I wondered why I was so sick — I didn't even drink that much (isn't that always our thought?).

I looked at a paper planner I used to track key dates, including my periods — mostly just to know when it was coming for planning purposes and to make sure I had tampons in my purse.

I flipped back one month, then another.

Holy shit, when was my last period?

I had no clue. Did I forget to write the last one down?

I went through my calendar and guesstimated that it was probably about eight weeks prior.

Holy crap, that makes me like three weeks late. That's bad. Very bad.

I sent Ryan to the pharmacy for some electrolyte sports drink and a pregnancy test. He brought home Gatorade and pregnancy tests — three of each.

One of the tests was digital, because you know, he's a tech geek and digital doesn't lie. The other tests were the kind where you spend twenty minutes holding it under different lighting to determine if you see a faint pink or blue line.

Plain as the dizziness in my head, all three screamed the same result.

Holy shit, I'm pregnant.

Now, I have to tell you that we weren't *trying* to have a baby. We had been married for five years by this point and simply decided to *stop preventing* pregnancy — as in throw out the pill and "see what happens."

Deciding to become a parent is scary as fuck. For years, Ryan would bring it up and I'd brush it off. He's a little over four years older than me and always cited his ticking biological clock as the natural reason for getting knocked up.

For a few years I'd quickly bounce between, "Hell no, I'm here to party," and "Yeah, a baby is a great idea." Also, thirty seconds after you get married, everyone feels it's completely appropriate to ask if you're thinking of having kids. I always just said, "Not right now."

Ryan wanted to make babies a few years into getting married. I tentatively said yes a few times but eventually chickened out and decided it wasn't the right time and stayed on the pill.

Fact is, I wasn't "ready" to have a baby, nor do I think I ever would have magically become ready. Maybe this was irresponsible of me, but we approached the whole thing with a half-accidental kind of attitude. I also wonder if I did this because when you commit, and then it doesn't work, you're let down. This way, I could leave it all up to some plan that was bigger than me.

That fall we had taken our first trip to Paris, and right around the time of our trip, I stopped taking the pill.

Do you know what happens when you stop preventing? Pregnancy happens. And for us, it happened very quickly.

After seeing the little blue plus sign of truth, I had a series of panic attacks.

How much did I drink last night?

Is this why I felt like throwing up halfway through my medium-rare steak dinner with my work team?

And, oh crap, I had my wisdom teeth out a few weeks ago — all four of them — was put on anesthesia, and then was on some potent painkillers.

Ugh, and the final realization — we were supposed to go to Ryan's company party that night. The last thing I wanted to do was go out, socialize, and attend events with my new friends, sobriety, and sparkling water. Not to mention getting used to being pregnant and growing a human.

Naturally, his company dinner was at a super-fancy sushi restaurant: raw fish for days.

I knew I wasn't "supposed" to eat raw fish or drink, but heck, I had been drinking the night before — *what's one more night?* I ate the sushi, had a few sips of wine, and then we told our family the next day.

The birth unplan

Nothing indeed prepares you for the change motherhood hurls at you. Nothing prepares you for pregnancy, either.

I was also one of those women who did not enjoy pregnancy. The only plus sides I discovered were gorgeous, thick hair, big boobs (but that excitement goes away when your stomach sticks out beyond), and people being extra nice to me.

There were plenty of negatives: the extra fluid, the farting, and for me, some random fainting — which happened at the office one morning while mid-conversation with a colleague. I'm lucky he was there to stop my pregnant ass from hitting the floor after I smacked my head on the desk and started to slump in my chair. I headed straight to my doctor's office, and everything was okay.

Other than the fainting, I'm grateful to have had a very healthy first pregnancy.

I was so ready for my baby to be out of my body. It was August, it was so damn hot, and I was carrying fifty extra pounds, hoping that this baby would weigh like forty and I'd only have ten to lose later. No such luck. He weighed seven pounds and five ounces. The rest, I was convinced, was in my (now ginormous) boobs.

All the expecting mothers in the Facebook groups seemed to have meticulously detailed birth plans. *My water will break when I wake up after a restful sleep, I'll sip my tea and labor at home until going to the hospital, then I'll slip into this designer robe when we check into labor and delivery. Also, I want unscented soy candles, massage oil, and a playlist of these thirty specific songs.*

I was not that kind of planner. Having watched those birth stories on TV, I saw what a complete shit show most births ended up being. And all that planning felt like *work*. I had a full-time consulting job. I also ate a bag of gummy worms every day like it was my job, so who had time for birth planning?

During an early visit with my OB, he asked Ryan and I if we were going to take any birthing classes.

Ryan asked, "Will classes change the outcome?"

The doctor thought for a second. "Nope."

Ryan and I looked at each other and shrugged — "Then no, we won't take classes."

This laid-back approach worked for us. And if you have kids, you know that they give zero shits about your "plans" anyway.

The only part that scared me were the drugs. When I had my wisdom teeth out, the surgeon prescribed Vicodin. Just one dose and I lay on the couch drooling, feeling as if I was levitating out of my body. I rarely even took Tylenol. Also, I wanted to be one of those badass moms that said, "…and I did it all without drugs."

The due date came and went — by more than a week. My OB scheduled me for an induction, which I was super anxious about. Google didn't help, as I read story after story of women being induced and then ending up with a C-section anyway. *C-section* seemed like such a dirty word, and I was determined to avoid it at all costs.

I really hoped that my water would break instead and tried everything that Google said to induce labor naturally — eating tons of pineapple, walking, bouncing on a yoga ball. I walked all day long, and when I wasn't walking, I'd eat pineapple on the yoga ball. They also suggested sex, but with fifty extra pounds and occasional fainting spells, this was *not* going to happen.

It turned out I didn't need the induction after all because of another problem — I needed a C-section. When I showed up for what was supposed to be my last appointment, my OB didn't like some things he saw during the exam and scheduled me for a C-section the next morning. I went home, ordered extra-spicy shrimp pad thai for dinner, and noticed some light bleeding right after. I called the doctor, who told me to pack a bag and head down to the hospital, where he was already on-call.

Holy shit, what's happening? Actually, in those moments, I was more worried that something was wrong than I was about the C-section. I didn't think there was supposed to be blood.

Ryan was pale. I was shaky and had no idea what was going to happen next. My mind was running all kinds of scenarios during the twenty-minute drive downtown.

After some hookups and testing, there I was laying all Jesus-on-the-cross-like on the C-section table. My arms stretched out to my sides, staring up at the lights. All I can recall was how cold and scared I was. After the spinal, it's common to feel extremely cold. Like a bone-chilling, shaking cold. I couldn't stop shivering.

That entire evening was a blur, even the surgery. After making what I'm assuming was the incision, the doctor asked me, "Are you ready?"

Well, actually no, I'd like to get a Big Mac, large fries, and a Diet Coke first — all supersized.

A little tugging and Jacob was here.

Pipes work!

"Pipes work," the OB announced as Jacob peed all over him. Jacob still giggles when I retell this story today.

He announced his height as twenty-one inches. "He's tall!" the doctor exclaimed.

Instinctively, I quipped back from behind the C-section curtain, "Must take after his mom," and the whole OR burst out laughing.

Well, I'm sure glad we didn't waste our Saturdays in birthing classes — no class would have prepared us for this. *This* prepared us for this.

It was somewhere around two o'clock in the morning when I was out of the monitoring room. All I wanted to do was eat something — but the doctor said I'd have to wait until the next morning. As they were moving Jacob and me to the room I'd call home for the next few days, I started feeling an allergy attack coming on. My eyes were watery, and my nose was stuffed up — I figured it was just my seasonal allergies flaring up. "Can someone get me a cool cloth?" I asked. I just wanted something to ease the irritation. The nurse wasn't so convinced that all I needed was a washcloth. I was oblivious.

In a few seconds there were suddenly more people in my

room.

Ryan filled in these blanks for me later. There he was, holding our hours-old new baby, and the nurses quickly wheeled in the crash cart. He later told me about his panic, his feeling that this couldn't be happening. I was so out of it that none of it even registered for me in the moment. They gave me a dose of Benadryl, and the reaction calmed down. It turned out that I was having a severe reaction to a painkiller, Naproxen, they gave me post–C-section. I had never had it before because it wasn't available in Canada while I was growing up. Well, that's good to know, and something I certainly couldn't have planned for.

Back in our room, which was like the Hilton of delivery recovery rooms, I was set up on the eighth floor with a view of Lake Michigan; the nurses would take Jacob to the nursery and only brought him back to my room when he woke up, which was right on time every three to four hours to nurse. I slept well in the hospital — *I could totally get used to this,* I thought.

Ryan would travel back and forth from home, where he was looking after the dogs. Jacob and I would hang out in my hospital bed and watch the sun rise over the lake each morning. I relished this alone time with my new baby. It was so incredibly relaxing. I had the best nurses and the best help. I was allowed to stay for four days with our insurance, and I did. Even though I could have left after three with the doctor's clearance, I wanted one more night.

One more night for me to have the help of nurses before I had to figure this whole thing out at home — alone.

The early days at home were a blur of bare boobs, books, and binkies. Between the lack of sleep, constant feeding, and incessant Googling every weird poop, sound, and rash, I found enjoyment in our daily walks on the beach. We lived in the Rogers Park neighborhood of Chicago, right on the shore of Lake Michigan, and every morning, I'd slide Jacob into the baby carrier, walk to Starbucks for a soy latte, then walk back, dip my feet into the water, and feel the sand between my toes. Having a baby in Chicago during the summer absolutely had its advantages.

Babies change your body, your brain, and your entire being. In the many months after having Jacob, I learned that there was no such thing as getting back to my old life. Motherhood taught me to create an entirely new life for myself. If someone had told me this before I got pregnant — *you'll create a new life* — I'm not sure I would have thrown caution to the wind the way we did. There was nothing wrong with my old life, why would I change it? Sure, there were hints of our old life in this newer, bigger one. Ryan and I continued to go out, mostly with Jacob nearby in the stroller or car seat. It often took more planning, like making sure the diaper bag was packed with extra diapers, bottles, blankets for spit up, and snacks for my raging appetite. I was hungrier when nursing than I was when pregnant.

We made sure to train him from a young age to handle dinner in nice restaurants and sometimes noisy sports bars. Yes, we were *those* parents who brought their baby everywhere.

On paper, we were doing a great job as parents. Beneath the surface though, I was struggling. First, I'm convinced that every new mom goes through postpartum depression — so many, in fact, that it needs a new, more positive name. I never said this out loud. I was strong, and I could handle anything. Soldier on, warrior!

So many moms talked about wanting to sit and cuddle their new babies all day long. I found new motherhood so incredibly tedious and boring. I wanted to do things. I wanted to pass the baby off so I could make dinner or fold laundry. I wanted to go back to work. I craved interaction with the adult world outside of other new moms. The other moms at the park seemed to talk about two things — their kids' accomplishments (my baby rolled over at two months!) and how much their husbands annoyed them (ugh, why doesn't he just read my mind?). This kind of small talk exhausted me more than being up half the night.

Of course, I loved Jacob fiercely, but it took me about eight months to feel that connection that everyone spoke of. That instant in-love feeling was not my experience. I felt like there was something wrong with me. *Do I love my baby enough? Am I any good at this? Am I a bad mom because I just want to go to work?*

The company I worked for had a generous maternity leave for the US — I ended up with about four months off work, completely paid. I kept in touch with my work colleagues while I was at home, dropped in with the baby to meet them for lunch, and met them (sans baby) for happy hours. I couldn't wait to jump back in and rock this new role — working mom.

Returning to work was much harder than I thought. I didn't miss my baby all day like some new moms said they did (more guilt) but it was the intense running around — packing for the day, dropping him off, getting to work, working, getting home, rushing dinner, unpacking the baby bag, washing bottles, and doing it all over again. I'd thought the newborn days were exhausting — working motherhood was no joke.

I was also in a period of my professional life when I was constantly proving myself. My inner narrative wanted me to be an even better employee than I was before kids. I wanted a badge that said I did it all and I was hot, smart, and a significant contributor to the household income. Well, that badge has many price tags to go along with it. And no one actually hands you the damn badge either.

I mean, I didn't even really *like* my job that much. It was fine, but I wasn't changing lives. I was a management consultant working as a project manager on huge federal government projects. I always thought a job was something that defined me. I was a mom now, and my work was *okay* — I didn't love it, but wasn't that normal?

Here I was, new mom, meh job, and no idea that I could, or would do more — so much more.

Growing pains

Two or so years later, I was pregnant again, and just like the first time, we had stopped preventing it. The unplanning planning method worked well for us the first go.

I didn't know if I was "ready" for another baby. I wasn't exactly ready for the first. We were in a groove by now, though. Jacob was two; he was sleeping and I was sleeping, which meant I was happy. He was still shitting his pants — no early potty training for this kid. I was enjoying wine most evenings (one of my favorite hobbies.)

What the hell was I doing introducing another baby? Why on earth would I want to go back to being up all night or turning into a human milk machine?

I felt okay during this pregnancy. I celebrated my thirtieth birthday while pregnant. It wasn't exactly how I had planned to spend this milestone birthday, but often these things don't care about our plans. For this big birthday I'd imagined a kid-free weekend, maybe back in Paris, devouring baguettes in the Champs de Mars, or sitting poolside in Vegas with a frosty glass of champagne. Or even a small introvert-friendly party with a dozen friends, who would all bring me gift bags filled with wine and chocolate.

Well, the only gift I got that year was chocolate.

A few days after my birthday, I went to the twelve-week ultrasound. Ryan was going to meet me there as soon as he could. I arrived at my appointment early, and he was still on the way. This was in Canada (yes, we threw an international move in there too), and for some reason, in Ontario, they don't allow the partner into the ultrasound room. It felt very odd to me. But those were the rules, and Canadians don't question the rules.

Knowing what was in store this time, I was excited to get to hear the heartbeat and see that little bouncy bean jumping around.

The ultrasound tech was eerily quiet. At first, I thought she was rude and lacked bedside manner. I couldn't see the screen so I scanned her face for clues. She was silent the entire time. Moving the slick ultrasound wand around and clicking her computer mouse.

Then she stood up abruptly, headed for the door, and said, "Your doctor will be in touch."

"What?" I asked, confused.

I was bewildered when she wouldn't give me any details.

"Do you have any details? How's the baby? Can I see the ultrasound? Can I hear the heartbeat?"

During my first ultrasound with Jacob, I got to listen to the heartbeat and watch the little bean bounce around. I needed this confirmation, this reassurance that everything was okay.

She didn't say a word, though — and she didn't have to. I could read it on her face.

Something was wrong. I was not leaving the ultrasound room without an answer.

"Is there something wrong with the baby?" I asked.

Quickly she responded, "I can't say."

I was frustrated. I realized that she wasn't a doctor and probably wasn't allowed to break any news to patients. But I also knew that I was not leaving with all these unknowns. *Do they really expect a pregnant lady to just go home without any conversation about the first ultrasound?*

I had to get creative. I didn't want to say the words, but I felt like I didn't have a choice. I needed to know. "Are you not allowed to say what I think you're trying to say?"

She nodded.

"Is there a heartbeat?"

She shook her head. "It stopped growing a few weeks ago."

Why didn't my body know this?

"The doctor will be in touch with your options," she repeated.

Then she turned and left the room.

Stunned and numb, I got dressed and left the exam room and exited to the lobby.

As soon as I busted through the doors, I called my mom and told her, choking out through my tears, "It doesn't have a heartbeat, it stopped growing at seven weeks."

After she offered a few comforting words, I saw Ryan pull up outside the building.

I greeted him and fell apart.

I didn't want to get in the car and go home. I felt frantic, out of place. I didn't know what to do.

Letting him hold me up, I said, "Let's just walk," not really leaving any room for discussion.

I held his arm. I felt fragile, broken. I had a dead baby inside of me. What the fuck? I felt like my body was broken. *What the hell is wrong with my body?*

We walked until we reached the end of the sidewalk. Realizing we couldn't walk any further, we turned around, got back in our cars, and headed home.

First, I stopped and bought a gigantic bottle of wine and some chocolate. I picked up Jacob from daycare without saying a word. I got him home and hugged him so hard. If I was meant to have one kid, then that was perfectly fine with me.

I referred this kind of symptomless miscarriage to as a "silent miscarriage." The doctor called that evening to explain my options. I sat on the couch, listening, feeling empty. My body didn't miscarry on its own, so I could take a special pill to induce miscarriage, or I could have a D&C — a surgery to clean it all out. The pill sounded like the least invasive, quickest, and unfussiest option, so I went with that.

I took the pill that night before bed and woke up to the most excruciating pain of my life. It was a pain worse than healing from the C-section and left me curled up in a ball on the floor of the dining room. After an hour or so, I had an urge to "empty out." I barely made it to the bathroom, and the remnants of that unsuccessful seed fell out with surprising force.

As soon as that happened, the pain faded, and I felt lighter. It was gone, I was empty again and alone. This whole painful ordeal lasted an intense twenty-four hours. I was eager to put the whole event behind me.

But it turned out I hadn't. More than a month later, I discovered that a portion of tissue was still growing (disgusting). What I *thought* was my period again turned into bleeding through my pants for two days.

I called my doctor. Bleeding through your pants isn't normal. And after all that, I needed to have a D&C anyway to get all the tissue from the pregnancy tissue cleared out. Maybe this was a lesson to choose the seemingly more difficult path first because this would have actually been the easier way.

Almost two months after that quiet ultrasound, I checked into the hospital for the procedure on a Friday morning. I still felt the sadness that my body failed me and was impatient to get on with life.

Even if I had tried to plan this whole thing, my plan would have been completely useless. This was not at all what I expected to happen — how could I? I had one pregnancy previously, which worked out fine, I welcomed a baby, then gave up sleeping. The idea that something would go wrong or not work out perfectly didn't even enter my mind. Though, this was another lesson in trusting that whatever happens *is* perfect.

I was grateful to leave that chapter behind me. I didn't know when I'd be ready to even think about getting pregnant again after this ordeal. I was emotionally exhausted and didn't know if I could handle the stress of another pregnancy, or worse, another miscarriage.

Untrying a third time

When it came time to get pregnant again, we resorted to our tried and true "untrying" method — but this time I knew how quickly I could get knocked up. And by this time, I knew it days before I took a pregnancy test. My swollen and tender boobs were a telltale sign. I waited until my period was due, then went out and bought three pregnancy tests — you know, to be sure.

Having had one healthy pregnancy and one miscarriage, I obsessed over what this third pregnancy would bring. Would I be like so many women I heard about who had multiple miscarriages before having a healthy baby? How many times would I have to try again?

I was completely happy and incredibly grateful to have one healthy child. *Who am I to want another one? Is that greedy? Also, why do I want to mess with my sleep?*

Every time I went to the bathroom, I held my breath, looking for blood. One day I had some spotting and messaged Ryan. He asked, "Does that mean game over?" I guess I wasn't the only one waiting for the other shoe to drop.

For the twelve-week ultrasound, I had to go back to the same clinic. Ryan came with me this time. I was a nervous wreck leading up to the ultrasound, especially knowing that I was heading back to the same place where I found out that I was going to miscarry.

Walking through the clinic doors, changing into the hospital gown, I felt like I was going through the motions. I was shaky with fear as those old emotions flooded back.

The ultrasound tech worked her magic wand while I held my breath, staring at the ceiling. I didn't want to see her face. If there was something wrong, I wanted to hold out hope just a little while longer that this was a good one.

"We have a heartbeat!" she declared.

I breathed the biggest sigh of relief. This bean was sticky. It stuck! The baby was healthy, and I could finally relax — a little.

Well, this pregnancy was easy-breezy. No fainting with this one, but I did have three bouts of food poisoning. All three were from eating sprouts of some variety from my local farm share box.

The first time was around twenty weeks, and I wondered, who gets morning sickness halfway through, and why am I puking in the middle of the day instead of the morning?

That would be the sprouts and not morning sickness.

I was much more relaxed during the second healthy pregnancy. We didn't take a birthing class this time either. I didn't obsess over every morsel of food. And by this time, I was also eating a plant-based diet so I didn't have to worry about undercooked meat or cold cuts. We went plant-based pretty much overnight after an ear, nose, and throat specialist wanted to take Jacob's tonsils out — more on this later.

At the twenty-week ultrasound, we found out we were having a girl.

Turns out the presence of a penis is the only way to figure out the baby's sex during an ultrasound: penis or no penis. Well, I was convinced that I was having a boy. I had been pregnant with a boy first, so naturally, I'd end up with two, right? I also had heard many stories about people who thought they were expecting a girl, but they simply couldn't see a penis, so they assumed it was a girl. I ended up paying for one of those creepy-looking 3D ultrasounds just to be double sure before we painted the bedroom.

Having been through one C-section, I knew what to expect this time. And since this one was scheduled, I had a date on the calendar and could prepare for the whole thing. This pleased my inner control freak. Though the actual surgery this time was crazy fast. Before I even knew what was happening, there was crying. Holy crap!

Talia had bright strawberry-blonde hair. Where did that super blonde baby come from? I mean, I've always been kinda-sorta blonde, though who knows what my natural hair color looks like anymore? Ryan hinted at a little *what the fuckness, is that mine?* In a joking, but not joking kind of way. He had golden blonde hair as a kid too, and now, with dark brown (and gray) hair, and brown eyes, they initially looked unrelated. Later though, you could look at her and see Ryan's face in hers.

She was the healthiest of babies, slept well, ate well, and hardly fussed. I blame my chill AF attitude throughout and the few weekly sips of wine I started enjoying in the second trimester. Maybe you're horrified reading this. A happy and relaxed mom has happy and relaxed kids.

This healthy, plant-based kid didn't touch antibiotics until she was six — then we discovered she was allergic to them — the antibiotics, not veganism.

Introducing a second kid also introduced exponential chaos. Leaving the house was a much bigger deal now that we had to plan around two nap times and mealtimes. Jacob had just turned three when Talia arrived and was barely potty trained. Seeing this new, wiggly thing in diapers must have been his permission to slide back into old habits. He continued having accidents for months after that. I had to be prepared with snacks for Jacob, extra clothes in case of a pants-crapping, plus all of Talia's gear. Getting two kids into the car would leave me sweaty and exhausted every time. I'd always wonder, is going out worth all this fuss? Sometimes it was. Many times it wasn't, and we'd have to leave story time, the bookstore, or the coffee shop after all the meltdowns.

I'd wanted two kids, and getting Talia out was easy-peasy thanks to the designer zipper installed in my uterus. I was done making babies now. I didn't have any pangs of sadness when Talia outgrew her newborn-sized diapers, her crib, or her baby clothes. I happily sold or donated every baby item as Talia outgrew it. I felt guilty for that too. So many moms want time to slow down. I wanted it to go faster so I could get to know the new humans living in our house.

IV. EMBRACING THE UNFUSSY LIFE

"Life is really simple, but we insist on making it complicated."

Confucius

We have two choices when we bump into something we don't like — accept it or change. Some of life's biggest and most stressful changes — from cross-country or international moves, to drastically changing your eating habits, to having kids, to how you deal with death — they all teach us how to become more us. This is about choosing an unfussy attitude when all you really want to do is throw a temper tantrum (which I still sometimes do).

Death bothers us because it reminds us of our own mortality

Driving into work on a bleak Chicago January morning, I was feeling a little groggy, so I treated myself to a hazelnut soy latte on my way in. I knew it was going to be a long and busy week. We were rolling out a new intranet at a huge health-care company, and I was in charge of communications.

I had no idea how long the week would soon get.

I walked into the office around 7:00 a.m. after a forty-five-minute commute. I'd said good morning, plopped my latte down on the desk, and unpacked my computer when my phone started buzzing.

It was my dad. He had just called the night before asking if we'd fixed the furnace. I figured he was calling again because he found a new reason why we should replace my furnace immediately, and perhaps some more information about carbon dioxide.

I put the phone to my ear.

It had nothing to do with the furnace.

"Hi, Dad."

"Vavó died."

"What?" I responded, confused. Like I want him to say it again, but not really. "What happened?" was all I could muster. Shocked and unprepared, I hadn't rehearsed this one in my head.

She was healthy as far as we knew. She was ninety-one and had a hopping social life — drinking tea with friends, going to church, and praying daily in her Jesus room. If she thought it was time for you to pray about something, she had a special prayer and a Catholic totem for that.

In her ninety-one years, she experienced a lifetime of changes. She'd immigrated to Canada with two young boys and had a third boy eight years after the second. As I looked at her life, I saw she was someone who experienced change, rather than created it.

Yet, when it was time for change to happen to her, she prayed, and from my perspective, always handled it with grace.

The only time I saw her angry was at my vavô's viewing, seven years earlier. We knew his death was coming. I was twelve weeks pregnant with Jacob. He had fought lung cancer — attributed to being around too much pigeon shit and painting cars at the Ford factory. Near the end of the three-hour viewing, it was time to close the casket. The family all stood around his tall, shell of a body, and my vavó, in all black, clutching one of her many rosaries in one hand and soggy tissues in the other, angrily shook her fist at him and was muttering something in Portuguese through her clenched jaw. I couldn't make sense of what she was saying (I only learned a few key Portuguese phrases).

This scene shook everyone, including me. I got emotional — and when she noticed my tear-filled eyes, she turned her whole body, looked up at me (I stood at least a foot taller than her as an adult), and said, fiercely and sternly, "You no get upset. You have baby. You look after you." It wasn't like she was lecturing *me;* she was lecturing my *soul*.

Nodding through tears, I told her, "I know, I know. I will."

My response wasn't convincing, and she asked me again. I bit my cheeks to force the tears to stop, realizing that if I stopped crying, she'd believe I was okay.

When my vavô was dying, I got the call from my dad that he

was in palliative care. "But don't worry about coming up," he said to me about my instinct to hop on the next plane from Chicago. He said the same thing when my vavô died too.

I ignored his pleas both times. The pull to be there was too strong. I knew I couldn't "do" anything, that wasn't the point. I urgently needed to be with my family. I wanted to be around them, near them, and feel them all in my presence. Being several hours away wrenched my gut in knots.

I feel incredibly lucky to have had a grandmother in my life as long as I did — and that my kids will remember their great-grandmother — they were seven and four at the time she died.

Immediately, I felt the uncontrollable need to pack up my stuff, hop in the car, and head straight there. Do not pass go, do not stop at the border (well, I would of course stop at the border) — and just go.

I didn't quite do that — there was the big launch at work that I was in charge of, family, logistics, and all. But I did leave the next morning, packing up the kids and heading out for an eight-hour drive. Ryan had some stuff to take care of at work, so he booked a flight a few days later to meet us there.

The kids had experienced the death of two of their dogs and one of their goldfish in the previous years. So they had suffered some loss from death. However, this was the first family death for them.

I had a lot of uncertainties.
How do I tell them?
Will they get upset?
Should they come to the funeral?
Can they handle the viewing?
What should we do at the viewing?
Should I let them see her body?

I trusted my gut and was open and honest about as much of the whole event as I could be.

That evening, when I told the kids, they got upset. And not because they were necessarily upset about their great-grandmother, but because it upset me as I verbalized what was happening. I wanted to get the words out carefully — this was important, and I wanted to use my words wisely.

Each kid handled the events of the next few days differently. Jacob, who was seven, kept his distance, asked a few questions. Talia, at four, was very curious and had many, many questions. At the viewing, she wanted to go up and see Vavó several times and touch her hand. She wanted me to touch her first. I didn't particularly feel the need to but did it anyway to show Talia it was safe.

"It's not scary," I told the kids. "The body is just a shell — a former house for the soul. A place where her consciousness used to live."

Ryan's flight was canceled due to a snowstorm, and at the last minute, he couldn't make it up. He talked to the kids about death again when we got home, echoing all the things they'd heard from me over the previous few days. We discussed how people get sad and upset when people die. Then he said something that made me pause.

"People only get so upset when someone dies because it reminds them of their own mortality."

I didn't necessarily agree. Also, as a Libra, I'm able to see all sides to an argument (fun for you if you're ever arguing with me).

Since my vavó lived until ninety-one, she experienced a long and full life. My dad's youngest brother and his son lived with her, so she got to see her family every single day. Living until the age of ninety-one feels juicy — sign me up for that, please. But are ninety-one years enough? Could she also have been fulfilled at eighty? What about forty-five? I wonder if I'm even pondering the right questions.

It's a reminder that we, too, will all die.

Of course, I *know* I'll die. Someday really far into the future, after all the people I love go, on some elusive "someday" when I'm 108, and sipping a twelve-dollar bottle of wine.

It could also be later today. Or next week. Or next month.

It's a grim reminder when we're not living our lives the way we want to be, and it's God's little way of kicking us in the balls to wake us up.

I was curious. Is that really why I was upset?

Was I upset because seeing death reminds me of my own — is this true? When someone dies, we're not sad for them. We're sad for ourselves; we feel sad when we think about the loss of people closest to us.

We realize it could be us, or someone else we love. Any day. Any minute. The next inhale might not come.

Then we start questioning how we're spending our time and how we're interacting with people. How we're harboring resentments and hate — and for what?

We didn't make it up to visit the family, including my vavó, for Christmas the year she died — one of my favorite holidays with my grandparents growing up.

Regret crept in when the thought entered my mind that I should have gone up that year. Something was pulling me there, that place of regret and resentment. Except I didn't go.

Would living with this regretful thought serve me? Would it change anything? Could I find a good reason to keep thinking this way?

No — I couldn't. So I let it go.

When we're reminded of our own death, we might say no to a project that doesn't excite us. We'll cuddle on the couch for an extra thirty minutes and let the dishes (and vacuuming and laundry) wait.

We're kinder. We're present. We live in the moment. What other way is there to live? Living in our pasts doesn't serve us, and constantly worrying about what could have or should have been doesn't serve us.

I started to write my thoughts about this, then put this piece down. Then, right before writing this chapter, something went flying out of my purse one morning. I looked around and couldn't see what it was. Later, when reaching for my hand cream to fix my dry, winter hands, I noticed something shiny and gold. It was one of my vavó's lapel pins — a gold dove. My uncle offered up some of her sweaters and coats to the family, and she had a pin on just about every sweater and jacket she owned. On chilly mornings, when I put on one of her sweaters, I feel connected to her. I think, *hi, Vavó.*

I picked this piece of writing back up and committed to finishing it.

The gold pin is my memento mori — a symbolic reminder of the inevitability of death — "remember death." Always, remember death.

It's a reminder to put the small, fussy things in perspective and refocus on the stretched-out timeline of our lives. A reminder to consider our values, desires, and big dreams.

Good things in all kinds of packages

At the time of this writing in 2020, we've moved eleven times in the sixteen years since we said, "I do." We've also bought and sold homes on at least half of those occasions. Our pattern looks like this — new state, upsize, new state, downsize, new country, upsize, new country, downsize, upsize, new state. "Settling" hasn't yet become a part of our pattern.

There's no change like picking up and moving. Many say moving is one of the most stressful events of your life, but perhaps I'm immune because it really doesn't bother me all that much.

A few months after we got married, Ryan attended a training near Boston and met someone from Indianapolis who mentioned a job opportunity for him. We had been married a few months, were waiting on my work authorization papers, and still had no idea when they'd come through.

Moving wasn't even on our radar. Well, Ryan didn't hear correctly and thought the job was in *Annapolis* — "Oh, that's not far," he said. When he realized we'd potentially move to *Indianapolis*, he hesitated but was open to the Midwestern adventure. I had already left Toronto to live in upstate New York, so what was a little move a few states to the west?

They flew us out to meet the team. Ryan, being a typical New Yorker, had to pull up a map to pinpoint where Indianapolis was. I rolled my eyes and thought, *damn yanks*.

We had a great time in Indianapolis. It seemed like a cute little town to live in, and they offered Ryan the same pay he was making in Manhattan. We calculated the cost-of-living savings, the five hours a day he wouldn't spend commuting, the knowledge that we had no idea when I'd be allowed to work in the United States, and committed.

Within a month, we sold the Poughkeepsie condo, packed up a moving truck, and headed West to Noblesville, Indiana, just outside of Indianapolis. We moved into a cute three-story apartment complex, sight unseen. After what felt like the world's longest drive, we arrived at 10:00 p.m., twenty-four entire hours after we left. The apartment was just as great as the pictures we'd seen — woo hoo!

We thought we were going to call Indy home for a while, so just six months into Indiana living, we bought a house we thought we'd grow into in a cute neighborhood of young professionals right across the street from the Indianapolis Colts' training camp. It was a two-story, three-bedroom home, and we talked about filling it up with kids — two of them to be precise.

By this time, I had my work permit and US travel documents — freed to travel and work. I was more excited about earning an income again than traveling. And the travel documents arrived just in time for our big wedding in Canada that fall. It had been almost six months since we'd been married, and housewifery was wearing on me. The day I received my work permit, I spammed all the job boards with my résumé (which was ready to go) and landed a job within days. My first job was at a tech college, reviewing their online programming for spelling, grammar, and usability. It was a temporary job, and I was a natural at it, so they offered me a full-time position. I tentatively said yes (because money) and kept searching for something better. (That I took this job and excelled at it could have told me then that I would eventually become a writer, but apparently, I wasn't ready to hear it at that point.)

One afternoon, I got a call from a recruiter who was looking for a management consultant to review financial claims for leaking underground fuel storage tanks. It took me a month to wrap my head around the job, but I figured it out, made great friends, and discovered there were great opportunities for growth and ladder-climbing. Finally I had my first American ladder to climb!

Boredom started to settle in after a little over a year of living the small-town Indianapolis life. We jumped into suburban life perhaps several years before we were ready. When we realized that rushing into another mortgage, extra bedrooms, and landscaping felt like too much responsibility, we knew we needed a change.

Ryan was feeling a bit trapped by the job we had initially moved to the Midwest for. He worked in tech, which wasn't exactly a booming industry in Indianapolis. He quickly landed a job in Chicago through his network, and as it turned out, that's where my company was headquartered. My conversation with my managing director looked like this: "We're moving to Chicago, can I transfer?" It was a no-brainer for him: "We'd love to have you!"

After just a day of apartment-hunting in Chicago, we found a place in Wrigleyville — on the forty-second floor of a building with jaw-dropping views of Lake Michigan sunrises and the downtown core. Before leaving, we even found a new home for the cat that traveled with us from Poughkeepsie: Belle. She was an outdoor cat and wouldn't have enjoyed the walk off the balcony.

Adjusting to city life after prematurely living in suburbia was like visiting a carnival for the first time. So many things to see, gluttonous foods to devour, and nightlife! I'd never lived this close to nightlife before. This was my first experience living in the middle of a big city. Ryan spent about a decade living in

Manhattan after going to NYU, and while he swore off living there after 9/11, he appreciated the accessibility, ease, and cleanliness of Chicago.

Living just a few doors down from Wrigley Field, we enjoyed the city to its fullest. We spent one afternoon (into the wee hours of the morning) attempting to sample chicken wings and beer in every single bar on Clark Street. I have no idea if we succeeded.

After a year in our shiny high-rise, we decided it was time to buy a condo in Chicago. I was steadily climbing that shiny company ladder, and with two of us earning good corporate salaries and no kids, we had money to spend and didn't want to blow it all on rent (which I later came to realize is a perfectly smart move).

We discovered an eight-hundred-square-foot, fully rehabbed courtyard condo in the Rogers Park neighborhood. My favorite part was that it was right on the beach. We bought it in 2006, at the top of the market. *Buy high, sell low* would become our new motto. We moved in during the spring and got to enjoy a few great summers there before we decided to move to Canada.

We left Chicago in 2009 when the market tanked; the value of our home dropped about $100,000, Jacob was a year old, and I was laid off from that supposedly shiny job (more on this later). We did a short sale on our condo and decided to move in with my dad, who hadn't yet remarried at that point. He kept the house, so he had space for us to find our footing again.

Ryan, Jacob, our two dogs, and I lived with my dad and younger sister (who hadn't moved out yet) for a year until we bought a new construction townhome in a fast-growing Toronto suburb. Living with family again had its moments, but it was mostly fun — and with so many adults in the house, there was always good food on the table and live-in babysitters. Communal living definitely had its perks.

I imported Ryan as my spouse, and we enjoyed all the benefits of being Canadians — buying beer at the Beer Store, all the health care our enormous taxes could handle, and great roads and parks. Canada can keep Tim Hortons and poutine.

I thought this move to Canada was going to be for good. At the time, I really thought we were going to settle. We were within an hour of almost all my family members, and I was excited for regular Sunday dinners. Returning after getting married, adopting dogs, and having a baby — it felt like a dream to have a support network of family and friends after being the actual new kid on the block for several years in three states.

But a lot had changed in the seven years I'd been away. I thought I'd pick up where I left off with old friends and relatives. It turns out they were different — and I was different. We were starting over. I got in touch with some friends who I used to enjoy spending time with, and when we got together, we'd reminisce briefly, and then when we realized how much we'd have to catch up on, it all felt exhausting. The invitations to "catch up" dwindled, and we found ourselves bored again — seeing the same faces that would visit us regularly in Indy and Chicago too.

Turned out that living near family didn't mean we'd see all of them more. Everyone was always so "busy" — people's lives were overstuffed with obligations. Baby showers, weddings, travel, vacations — no one had time to do Sunday dinner anymore (except my mom and her new husband, my dad and his new wife, and my sister).

After only three years, Ryan had had enough of living in Canada. He wasn't enjoying having a lower salary than he'd earn in the US, combined with the higher cost of living — and did I mention the taxes? And even though Canada felt like home to me, it never felt right to him.

After four years in Chicago, and then three years in Canada, I never thought we'd return to the United States. Things change, situations change, and new opportunities arrive — lots of them as it turned out. As luck and opportunity would have it, we ended up with about a month to pack up and set out on our next adventure. Another international move, with two kids (who were then one and four), two dogs, and two working adults wasn't easy — but we did it.

We quickly moved into a condo in the up-and-coming West Loop neighborhood of Chicago. We were back in city life again: a thirteen-minute walk to work, walking everywhere with kids, public transportation, parks, festivals, the lakefront, and every food we could possibly desire. Even with two kids in tow, we were having fun!

We spent about a year in the Chicago condo, then we were ready to buy a home for our family of four. Jacob was in kindergarten, and we were realizing that as he and Talia were getting older, we'd need more space. Well, space in the city runs about a million bucks, so we looked to the 'burbs again. We settled on an acre in the woods south of Chicago. Well, we *thought* we'd settled.

We spent about five years there, including many hours cutting down trees, building a deck, renovation projects in both bathrooms and the kids' bedrooms, even acquiring more animals — a backyard chicken farm and some cats.

I never really felt at home in the Midwest. It was like being back in Indianapolis, where everyone seemed to have grown up there and already had their lifelong friends and family. Other than meeting some neighbors and families through the kids' sports and school, we were outsiders. It took a while to find our people there.

We were also looking for a change. The school situation wasn't as great as we thought — and the idea of moving to *another* Chicago suburb where we'd definitely have to spend more money and continue to be the outsider family wasn't appealing. We needed something different — it was time to shake things up again.

Where to next? We briefly home shopped just across the state border. We were only five minutes from northwest Indiana, where we'd find lower taxes but more expensive, cookie-cutter homes that looked directly into those of our possible neighbors.

After living in the woods, it felt super awkward to walk outside your front door to see your neighbors a few feet away.

We came close to putting in an offer on an Indiana home but just couldn't do it. We felt like we were settling for less. As in, not going after what we really wanted — great schools, great neighborhood, great sports and resources for the kids, and family too — was that too much to ask?

Out of the blue, Ryan had a job opportunity in Manhattan, with the executive team all living across the river in Jersey. So after five years in our country-feeling home, we had yet another big party to sell all our stuff. Within just a few months, we listed and sold our home (for a cash offer) and moved with only our two vehicles and a six by twelve trailer. We moved with almost nothing — planning to buy what we needed when we arrived in our New Jersey rental home.

At the time of writing this chapter, we have just bought what we're calling our seven-to ten-year home in New Jersey. With Talia in the third grade, and Jacob in seventh, it felt like time to settle — finally. Even though we thought we were ready to settle several times before — with and without kids. For real this time! *Maybe.*

If your head is spinning, here's a rundown of all the moves: I left Canada for Poughkeepsie, then on to two Indiana homes, two Chicago homes, into my dad's house in a Toronto suburb, to a townhome nearby, then back to Chicago, out to the Chicago suburbs, then on to two homes in New Jersey.

Having coordinated three international moves and all these state-to-state and even in-state moves, and now doing it with kids, animals, and property to buy and sell every time, I can confidently share how grateful I am for things like movers, selling all your stuff, and family that shows up to help on moving day.

If I hadn't said "yes" to Ryan when he popped the question, I'm not sure I'd be living this life of constant change and building resilience for myself and our family. I wonder if I would be one of those people who never leaves their hometown. Would I enjoy it there? Would staying in one place create an aversion to change?

The moves within the same town or a few towns over were just as much work, if not more, as moving to a new state or country. You can draw out a cross-town move over a month, moving a little at a time. It makes getting settled in your new home easier, but it feels like it takes forever. With long-distance moves, you don't have the luxury of making multiple trips. You pack it all once, and you unpack it all at once.

The big moves always felt like significant emotional moments. I cried when I left Canada for the first time. I cried when we left Chicago for Toronto; I sat in the car and cried with Jacob in the back before I could pull away. I cried again when we left Canada, now with two kids in the back of our shiny new minivan. Were we making a mistake?

Then finally, as we left Illinois in the spring of 2019 to move to the East Coast, we pulled out of the driveway in the middle of the night to start the thirteen-hour drive. Jacob, ten at the time, in the backseat of the car, and Talia, seven, in the back of the pickup truck with Ryan. I got out of the car to walk back through the empty house. There was no turning around to pick up "one last thing."

My footsteps echoed through the house. We'd thought this was our forever home, and after five years, we discovered it wasn't. A part of me was grieving this. I got back into the car, shut the garage door behind me, and slowly rolled down the driveway and out of our neighborhood. Knowing that after this move, we wouldn't be back. Deep heavy breaths, tears rolling down my cheeks. At first, I wanted to hide them from Jacob, who broke down in tears a day earlier after his last day of school. He had made a close friend there and was upset to leave his new friendship. I realized that hiding it was the wrong answer. It's perfectly okay to feel sad, and scared, and excited — and to let tears fall for those reasons, and any other reason.

Time will tell if all this moving served us well as a family and whether it will help or hurt the kids' resilience. We really want to give them a stable high school experience; we can only hope we're doing the best job we can with our current set of resources. And if we don't, we'll be keeping therapists in business.

I wonder if I'm built to live in a "forever home." When the kids move out, will they choose to live in the same town? Will they crave fewer changes in scenery? Or will they want to get as far away from us as possible?

We've designed a life now that we can move after them if they move away (haha kids!). Maybe we'll sell everything again and go all-in on a nomadic lifestyle. Only time will tell.

Less stuff, more life

Not long after our first downsizing, a popular vegan blogger shared a quote from Dave Ramsey: "We buy stuff we don't need with money we don't have to impress people we don't like."

That hit where it hurt. Who was I when you took away all my stuff? I was still me. Sitting alone with that thought can feel unbearable at first.

From the brand names on my clothes to the kinds of cars we drove — it all had a meaning. When the lease on our Kia Sportage ended, Ryan went out and came home with a new lease — on a Mercedes.

I didn't drive the car for a week. It just sat there. I drove the Dodge Ram we had at the time instead. *Who am I to drive a Mercedes? Am I trying to be fancy? Do I deserve this? Am I trying to impress people?*

I remember a time when I used to see people driving luxury cars and instantly judge them — who do they think they are? Now that was me — who did I think I was? I did some deep digging before I could drive the car. The first time I drove it, I actually felt the difference between a Kia and a Mercedes — okay, now I got it.

A few months later I discovered an old vision board — guess

who had cut out a glossy magazine image of the round Mercedes logo? That's right, me. I didn't remember doing it or even wanting one. Ryan went car shopping that day without me (that's just how he rolls) and unconsciously came home with the car that was on my vision board.

I think we can grasp the essence of not needing things to impress people when we feel detached from our things. As much as I enjoyed its better performance and comforts, I could trade that car back in for a Honda or a Kia and not give it much thought.

Whenever I'm on the phone with home insurance agents, and they offer additional protection to replace my "valuables," I reply, "No thanks, I don't care about my stuff."

They often rebut, "What about your TV? Artwork? Furniture?"

Nope. Don't care. It's all replaceable. Although, really, I probably wouldn't even replace a single piece of it. Looking around my home today, I don't see anything so fancy or valuable that it would attract a thief. Important papers are all in a safe and in the cloud. And all the meaningful things like note cards and special gifts are irreplaceable anyway — you can't assign a value to them.

By spending less time acquiring, handling, and cleaning (or hiring someone to manage) my things, there's more space for life to happen.

Less stuff also means less stress. Ever watch the A&E show *Hoarders*? When you see the first clip of a room full of trash, you're in shock. It feels stressful. Walk into your bedroom, and laundry is piled up higher than the bed — stress. Dishes overflowing in the sink — stress. Piles of mail to sort through — overwhelm!

The less stuff I have vying for my attention, the more at peace I feel.

Now, all this moving, downsizing, and upsizing didn't force me to restrict my belongings to a hundred items or pare down a shoe collection to a single pair of fake Birkenstocks. I keep a reasonable number of shoes and have just two purses — one that fits my laptop, and a cross-body bag.

When we downsized from our 1,700-square-foot suburban Indianapolis home to what was possibly the smallest studio apartment in Chicago at just 500 square feet, the only piece of furniture we took with us was our bed. To get rid of everything else, we hosted a "buy our shit" party (the actual invitation name). We invited all our friends and told them everything was for sale. I threw a small fit when Ryan sold a piece of (not expensive or fancy) artwork off the walls and felt a pang of sadness saying goodbye to my favorite rustic kitchen table with matching benches. I knew they were all going to good homes, though. And I quickly learned that I am not my things.

My furniture, paintings, all of it — was not me.

During our big garage sales, Ryan would get a wave of excitement seeing our home getting emptier as the wad of cash in his pocket grew thicker, and if I wasn't paying attention, he'd drag out some of the items we agreed we'd keep. I may have seen a for sale sign on the dogs.

I did accidentally sell his $900 guitar for $100 and some of his practically new tools for deep discounts. But the idea of lugging stuff around the country that would sit in a closet bothered me much more. Even if we put stuff in storage, I imagined the cost of a storage unit at conservative $80 a month for just a year — that's $960. When the cost to store it is the same or more than moving it, it's not worth it. Also, considering the environmental impact and costs to rent a bigger truck and pay for movers — it's all out of control for just a bunch of stuff.

The satisfaction I feel from using something completely, from a tube of toothpaste to a container of vitamins, might be totally unreasonable. I love useful stuff, and not just that, but things that have multiple uses. This means I got rid of single-use things like a garlic press, the chop-chop machine, and the apple slicer. A great knife will do all these tasks perfectly and take up less kitchen drawer real estate.

Once again, leaving Canada the second time, the hardest thing to say goodbye to was our amazing kitchen table. We'd found it at a local market; it was made of hundred-year-old barn board from Southern Ontario. I loved that table. It was a conversation piece, full of original mill marks, dents, and dings. We enjoyed many conversations over multiple bottles of wine with friends and family over that table. It had such character. I sold this one for more than we paid, though, so that eased the pain a little. Whenever we watched a buyer carry our kitchen table out the door, each move started to feel real.

After leaving Canada for the second time to head back to Chicago, we downsized again from a 2,200-square-foot townhouse to a West Loop condo with half the space. We were proud that the worldly possessions of two adults and two children could fit into a seventeen-foot U-Haul truck. We decided if we ever need a truck bigger than this to move, then we probably have more stuff than we need. To this day, that was still our largest moving truck.

Living in a small or right-sized space forced us to be more conscious of what we brought in. It's easier to see when your space is overrun with stuff when you have fewer places to stash things and forget about them.

Our furthest move distance-wise was when we moved from Illinois to New Jersey, and we brought the least stuff. We sold or donated some things, left others with the new homeowners, and trashed what we couldn't give away. We moved with almost no furniture — just my desk, two end tables, and a mattress. That was it for furniture. The rest was our clothes, a few household items (I got rid of the dishes too), and sports equipment.

Downsizing (or right-sizing as I call it now), our stuff felt so good. In our Jersey shore town rental, it was an adventure to sleep on air mattresses and sit on lawn chairs for a week while we shopped for new furniture. We needed to replace some of our growing kids' furniture anyway.

People think we're crazy getting rid of all our stuff. They say they couldn't imagine getting rid of everything. Now, giving my stuff away or selling it feels freeing to me. I don't get attached to stuff anymore — except maybe my desk and my many kitchen tables. Even then, I always find a new one to love.

I love a big bookshelf full of books like the next writer and book lover, but now you won't find many in my home. I used to arrange my books by spine color, and laying eyes on the rainbow made me smile every time. Except for one thing — those books just *sat* there. I rarely read a book twice. I might read a hard copy (paper books only, please) and then listen to the audio version later. Now, when I read a book I love, I recommend it to a specific friend and pass it along if they want it. If they don't, it lands in the donation pile.

There are entire television series dedicated to people's obsessions with their crap. Take *Tidying Up with Marie Kondo* on Netflix, for instance. The whole tidy-your-pile-of-garbage movement has to be equally as big as our consumption and collection problem. When can we be okay with being us — simply existing?

I watched the first two episodes with Jacob and Talia, and they were intrigued. Their little eyeballs were glued to the screen — to a show about people tidying up! Then they asked, "Can we KonMari our rooms?"

Pinching myself, I looked around the room to make sure I was awake, flipped the TV off, and said, "Sure!" And KonMari their rooms they did. Jacob filled a big garbage bag and found a perfect tidy little home for all his socks and underwear as well as every last Lego.

Ms. Kondo, if you read this — I have no idea what kind of magic you're oozing into Netflix, but it worked on my two kids. Thank you.

We're conditioned to want more, bigger, faster, and better. It can feel uncomfortable going against the grain and announcing, "we're downsizing," or "we're selling it all!" Especially when on the other side, we're growing our income and leveling up in our business and lives.

Well, we chose a different narrative. We've been Marie Kondo-ing our shit before it was cool.

I intentionally keep some cupboards and closets empty. I get deep satisfaction from opening a drawer to find it completely empty. It means I've left space for stuff to happen, things and experiences I couldn't have planned for. It's my way of telling the universe we're open for more abundance.

Less stuff also means more happiness. The less stuff I have competing for my attention — *look after me, use me, play with me, maintain me, update me* — the more I can tune into myself. Let go and let myself be happy. Having less stuff to look after, more money from not wasting it on junk, and more time and focus, because I'm not preoccupied with my things, lets me focus on the bigger things — meaningful work, enjoying my family, and most importantly, time for me.

When people give us looks like we're nuts, we shrug. "It's just stuff."

Contraction in one area and expansion in another. We have this idea of how the arc of adulthood is supposed to go — we acquire more things, kids, pets, houses, and money until we hit retirement and then the nest starts to empty and we start to downsize. Why do we need more shit as we get older? To prove we've made it? Made it where? We can't take it with us when we go — and it makes moving way more work.

Honey, I threw out the bacon

When Jacob was a toddler, he constantly had a stuffy nose and was always breathing through his mouth.

I thought a lot of kids were just mouth breathers, so I didn't think much of it. Then one winter, he had pneumonia twice, and a series of coughs that would last for a month or more. His tonsils were always red and swollen — I wondered how he could even swallow. He had a healthy appetite though and was gaining weight just fine.

Jacob's pediatrician referred him to an ENT (ear, nose, and throat) specialist who recommended removing his tonsils and adenoids and planting tubes in his ears. When I talked to family members and other moms about the suggestion, I discovered that this was an extremely common surgery.

But Jacob was only two years old. I couldn't fathom signing him up for elective surgery, especially because a tonsillectomy almost killed Ryan. Before we met, he had an elective tonsillectomy at twenty-two. He woke up at home one night after surgery choking on blood. The sutures had ruptured, and he was throwing up blood. A fast trip to the ER, where he passed out from losing so much blood, was followed with a blood transfusion.

Even though I wasn't there for this horrifying event, the story scared the hell out of me. There was no way Jacob was going to have surgery if he didn't need to. I was determined to figure out the cause of his problems and solve them in some other way. I'm no doctor, but I believe our bodies know how to heal when we give them the right support. For some reason, cutting out body parts we were born with seemed like complete insanity to me.

The ENT specialist couldn't tell me why his tonsils were enlarged. I'd ask, "But why are they so big?" He wasn't at all interested in investigating why. His response, "It's common in kids."

That is the opposite of an answer. We had his hearing checked to make sure it hadn't been damaged from sinus drainage. His hearing was perfectly fine — I knew he could hear me when I was telling him 'no' for the fifteenth time. He was simply being a toddler.

The ENT said I had two choices, put Jacob through surgery or take a wait-and-see approach.

He explained some kids grow out of it, and some kids just have enlarged tonsils. I couldn't accept this answer. At the very least, I'd wait and see.

There had to be a reason why he was constantly stuffed up. I heard about a naturopathic doctor who worked out of the massage clinic I visited to repair the knee I'd injured while training for a half marathon.

Right away, the naturopathic approach made so much sense. "We look at the whole patient, not just symptoms." Finally! Some hope!

She suggested that a food sensitivity could be causing his enlarged tonsils, so she recommended food allergy testing. She explained that the tricky part about identifying food sensitivities is that they don't always provoke an immediate reaction. I thought, no way he has any food allergies, he's never had a strange reaction to any foods, and I thought he was pretty regular — five healthy piles of regularity each day.

She recommended an IgG test. I had no idea what this was. I only knew about the kind of allergy testing where they scratch your skin with potential allergens and look for a visible reaction.

I learned that food allergies are a reaction to food proteins and can be immediate or delayed. I had associated food allergies with severe reactions, the ones that immediately result in itchy skin, trouble breathing, vomiting, throat swelling, or anaphylaxis.

IgG reactions, on the other hand, may take several hours to several days to present. Some common IgG reactions are headaches, hypertension, asthma, recurrent respiratory infections, joint pain, sinus infections, or weird skin rashes. Since IgG allergic reactions take hours or days after ingestion to appear, this makes it very difficult to pinpoint culprit foods.

We completed the IgG allergy test with a simple blood spot from a finger prick (Jacob barely flinched). Then they send the sample to a lab where it was tested against ninety-six of the most commonly eaten foods, and we received the results three weeks later. My insurance covered the test (this was Canada), which cost about $230. Even if I had to pay out of pocket, though, I wholeheartedly believe it would have been a valuable investment in his health.

I received the results in a well-organized report, which detailed what foods caused an immune reaction and the severity. Based on this report, the naturopath recommended removing trigger foods for at least three months, then reintroducing foods one at a time, a new one every week, and watching for any reaction. Jacob's reactions were typically a stuffy nose or more crapping.

The report revealed that Jacob was sensitive to cow's milk, cheese, and eggs, and somewhat sensitive to soy, asparagus, oranges, and cod. I immediately cut these foods out of his diet as best I could.

I noticed a change in just a few weeks. He could breathe through his nose and went from five shits a day to two.

Removing dairy from his diet ended up being our gateway drug to a plant-based diet.

I consulted with the same naturopath and told her about my recurring sinus infections — a few a year — regular tonsillitis, and stomachaches every time I ate yogurt.

I didn't even bother with testing. She suggested I avoid all dairy for two weeks, then reintroduce it to see how I felt. I went to the grocery store on the way home and bought soy milk, vegan cheese, and dairy-free ice cream. It was fine, and I never missed the stomachaches the cow variety gave me. I quit all dairy for a few weeks then tried a bowl of dairy ice cream. An hour or so after devouring that bowl of double chocolate chunk, I thought I was dying. My stomach was cramped in knots and my body was like, *WTF did you do to me?*

The easy choice was to stop eating dairy. Which also got me thinking. *If dairy comes from a cow, then what about the cow? Is eating animals even a good idea?* I went down the vegan rabbit hole. After reading a few books on the topic, I decided to give it a try.

There was no family meeting or discussion, I simply stopped buying meat. Since I did the cooking at home, Ryan didn't complain. He didn't complain either when his high blood pressure returned to normal and he no longer needed medication to control it.

After several months with these foods off his plate, Jacob's tonsils were visibly smaller.

He never went back to the ENT and went the next several years without antibiotics. I haven't had a sinus infection, or any need for antibiotics, in more than a decade. We'll all occasionally have some dairy-filled ice cream and pay for it dearly the next day.

Jacob still has selective hearing.

Sneaking shrimps over the kitchen stove

When I began to fully embrace the plant-based life, I was all in. I bought all the books, watched all the documentaries, and read all the food labels — and I preached to anyone who would listen.

I sometimes blame my lack of friends on my introversion, but really it was probably more related to me obsessing over plants. I was excited about everything I was learning so it was the only topic you'd find in my Facebook and Twitter posts. I never sat down with my omnivore friends and lectured them over medium-rare burgers, but if we got on the topic, it would be hard to shut me up.

When I'd go to vegan events, at first I'd be excited to get to eat all the vegan treats, but then I encountered people who were more vegan than me, and I'd find out I was doing vegan all wrong.

Oh shit, I didn't even think about my old leather shoes — should I donate them all now?

The steering wheel in my car is made of leather! Oh no! What about baseball gloves?

Honey isn't vegan? A bee is an animal?

Some folks in the vegan community were quick to shame

others if they weren't vegan enough. And I was never going to be vegan enough.

I fell into this trap too. I obsessed over every morsel of food — an obsession that became unhealthy because I'd stress about the food on our plates. I'd stress if Ryan was taking the kids out to eat and would get them regular ice cream. Stress does not do a body good.

This isn't a proverbial middle finger to vegans or a "you told me so" to omnivores — I love you, all of you.

We're constantly changing. Even if we say stuff like "things never change" they do. You just have to notice. My body has been a constant cyclone of change since conception. Sitting up, rolling over, crawling, walking, baby teeth, no teeth, brown (blonde?) hair, gray hair.

The way I work, the work I do, the way I talk, how I spend my money, my friends, my thoughts — everything changes. Always has, always will.

When we moved into our south Chicago home, the previous owners left a lot of stuff there. They thought they were being helpful, but the only things of real value were the books they left, especially *The Untethered Soul* by Michael Singer. I read it while on a kid-free Vegas vacation with Ryan.

As I was sitting poolside, cooling off with margaritas on the rocks, something in that book made me whip a notebook and pen out of my bag with wild determined force and start scribbling words like a madwoman. I riffed about change, life, learning, working, family, and finally, food.

Fuck it, I thought, when in Vegas! And I ate whatever the hell I wanted when we were there. No one would know.

We're supposed to always be changing. We're designed to change. Why should the food I eat stay the same?

Dairy-free, red meat–free, then plant-based, then oil-free, then raw vegan. The food was always "wrong," and I could always do so much better.

When I first went plant-based, I felt amazing. Then, BAM

— I felt shitty. Though it was less "BAM" and more slowly over time.

Something was off. I was craving oily foods, I was bloated, and my skin was angry at me. If I was going to preach to anyone who would listen about eating a vegan diet, then it had to feel good for me personally. I didn't feel healthy and it showed.

First, I started cooking with oil again. I put more cooked veggies on my plate and pushed the raw ones aside. I always kind of hated raw food anyway. I'm not a rabbit.

I doused my veggies with that EVOO (that's extra virgin olive oil if you're not a Rachael Ray fan). I practically bathed in it!

Then I started having wicked cravings for seafood. I'd never order it at a restaurant but would sneak it off the kids' plates. I was afraid of being judged. I had a vegan food blog, and though I was absolutely unknown in this space, I wondered if a reader would see me at a restaurant and want to know what I was eating and drinking.

Shit, I'd once posted a bottle of wine I was drinking on Facebook and a guy commented, "Here's a link to a list to find vegan wines." I know! Who would have thought some wine isn't vegan? Some wineries filter wine through something called isinglass, from fish bladders, or even gelatin, egg whites, seashells, and other animal products — making it not vegan-friendly. I went down the rabbit hole of learning what everyday products weren't vegan — crayons made with rendered cow fat; french fries fried in beef fat; tattoo ink made from charcoal that comes from burning animal bones; drinks with dyes made from insects. It's all fucking exhausting and extraordinarily fussy for me.

I was judged and I feared it. After a few months of this, I asked myself, why the hell do I have to hide what I eat? So I ate some shrimp and also gave up on guilt.

When I held cooking workshops and worked with clients, I always told them I didn't care what they ate. I was never judging.

Many folks used to come to my cooking workshops because they wanted to eat healthier.

Instead of judging them, I was judging myself.

Here's what happened when I stopped letting guilt about eating animal products affect me.

I became less of a bitch (in my opinion anyway), my skin cleared up, my digestion machine revved up, and I found writing easier.

Yes, I can't un-know everything I learned about how flesh gets to my plate. Today, I believe in eating with a conscience and at the moment, I eat mostly plant-based with seafood and the occasional burger or steak. And that will probably change too.

I had to make the unfussier choice and choose a new attitude based on what was most important to me — feeling good. If I don't feel good, what the heck is the point?

If I feel good, I'm happier, and if I'm happier, my family is happier. It's a win-win-win.

I still don't want to eat dairy, and gluten still gives me the farts.

When I stopped being vegan, I also stopped teaching cooking workshops and writing about food. It didn't light me up anymore, and I can't write about things that don't fuel me.

I have a theory on change when it comes to our health. We know we need constant change in our routines, our ways of thinking, and our exercise to keep sharp, to keep our body challenged. This is totally unscientific, but it's my gut-theory that we need to constantly change up how we eat too. (Reminder again that I'm not a doctor, so please check with your health professional before making changes.)

I really, really wanted to keep food — the most basic of necessities — unfussy, but sometimes my choices still sound fussy.

I published a blog post in 2014 titled "I'm not vegan anymore" and shared it with my then community. I was scared to publish the article. I wrote about how my tastes and cravings changed. It was an honest story about how I was judging myself for sneaking meat sometimes, and worse — feeling guilty about it. It was about my gut feelings on how our diets need to constantly change. Then, I got a little punchy around dealing with the vegan police and signed off, "Cheers, from the mostly plant-based, not judging, with a side of seafood, eat whatever the hell you want and be happy, unfussy chick. And for the love of God, stop letting food rule your life and stop the food shame!"

No one personally replied, they just unfriended me on Facebook and unsubscribed. They were there for the food, not the conversation, and that's okay.

Years later, Ryan would leave the house for coffee, end up at the local Tractor Supply Company for PVC pipe, and return with six chicks. He went back two weeks later for chicken feed and came home with two ducklings. I grew up in a suburb with a tiny backyard, and my exposure to chicken had previously only been with nuggets and wings. I knew nothing about farming.

When the kids incubated some of the eggs, we figured most wouldn't hatch. Well, we were wrong, and most *did* hatch. Our flock reached its peak at thirty chickens and four ducks.

I was eating meat again, but I couldn't eat the chickens from our backyard. A local rancher friend came over to show us how to process them. I hid in the bedroom. The kids grabbed popcorn and pulled up a chair.

I couldn't kill my own food with my hands, so I sure as heck had no right to eat any chicken now, right?

Jacob and Talia would snuggle the chickens and read them books when they were chicks. When Ryan explained this is where chicken wings come from, Jacob proclaimed, "I'm never eating anything with the word chicken in it ever again."

Until of course, his hockey team headed to Buffalo Wild Wings for lunch. Nugget what?

Talia, on the other hand, delighted in learning that to kill the chicken, you hang it upside down and chop its head off. She was four when she asked, "When do I get to chop their heads off?"

Proof that nurturing sometimes doesn't mean shit.

The thought of killing a chicken, a duck — or even a larger animal, like a cow or pig — myself, on purpose with my own hands, makes me shudder. I couldn't do it. I don't need to try to know this.

So should I pay someone else to do it for me? I feel like I'd be taking the easy way out and would be completely detached. From my food, from life, from myself.

Detaching is easy. And hey — if you can kill your dinner yourself, cook it, and eat it — all the power to you.

Our hens ended up being mainly for eggs; once they get too old the meat isn't good. We also lost a bunch of the flock to a fox, hungry racoons, and the neighbor's dog.

Whatever is on your plate — whether it's mostly plants, six pounds of lobster, a hot dog, or some bacon-wrapped sea scallops with a hint of lemon — you'll find no hint of judgment from me. I've been on all sides — eating them to not eating them.

When I run through the list of things I don't eat — it certainly sounds fussy. I still avoid dairy and gluten. I've gone back to the plant-based lifestyle here and there, and have many plant-based days, as well as the occasional water fast — but I enjoy food and wine more than the discomfort of fasting for now, so I'll stick with this way — until I don't.

But to keep it real about the most basic of necessities, my attitude about it needs to stay cool.

When life hands you a shit-sicle

When Talia was turning five, my mother-in-law and I were at Whole Foods with her, shopping for a birthday cake. We were almost finished when I looked down and noticed my purse wasn't hanging on the cart anymore.

My eyes darted around the store, and I did a super-fast retracing of my steps. It was gone. I was freaking out and ugly-crying on the inside, but I kept calm because Talia was watching, and I wanted to teach her that freaking out isn't a good way to solve problems.

I made my way to the customer service counter and alerted the helpful staff, who called the police to file a report. Twenty minutes or so later, when I started making calls to the card companies, the thief had already spent a few hundred bucks at some gas stations, a pharmacy, and a Target store. Then they had a hot dog lunch. A vision of someone choking on a hot dog came to mind.

Thankfully, my mother-in-law was there. She paid for all our groceries when I couldn't, and I used her phone to call the credit card companies and Ryan, who had to drop off the other key for the car — because mine was in my bag, along with my phone, work badge, and house keys.

It was a huge pain, but we replaced the locks to our house that afternoon. I replaced my driver's license and phone, alerted the credit bureaus, and moved on.

The police never found the thief, but they shared the video footage. I made Ryan watch it; I couldn't even look. The still images were enough for my imagination. Here's what I know — a man in a Chicago Bears jersey wandered around Whole Foods empty-handed for forty-five minutes. While I had one hand on my shopping cart and was reaching to grab something off a shelf, the man picked up my purse and carried it straight out of the door.

Once the taste of puke cleared up from my mouth, I forgot all about the video. I needed a new purse anyway. That was the moment when I switched to a cross-body bag.

Five months later, on Valentine's Day (our wedding anniversary), I was on the train heading home from my corporate job on our way out for dinner, when Ryan called me. "Why is there only a hundred dollars in the bank?"

Weird. I've been known to make some banking errors in the past, and maybe something cleared that I had forgotten about. I figured it was a mistake, and I'd just move some money around.

At the time, the bank wasn't able to give us any details, just that someone had withdrawn $3,462. The bank said it could have been an error, but we would have to wait until the next business day to get more details. To be safe, we put a hold on our account so that no money could go out, only in.

The morning after the withdrawal, we were able to download a copy of the withdrawal slip presented at the bank. When Ryan showed me the image, I felt sick. It was in my name, with a copy of my signature precisely as it appeared on my (stolen) driver's license, my bank account number, and my social security number written on the slip. What really stopped me cold was that my social security card hadn't even been in my wallet.

Once I stopped shaking, I went into action mode. Our first stop was to visit the branch where it happened. Oddly, the bank was in the lobby of the same building where Ryan worked at the time in Chicago. Making this discovery was scary — was this a targeted event? It turned out to be a coincidence.

We spoke to the branch manager and showed him the withdrawal slip image — which was from a branch in nearby Chinatown. He was floored. Writing a social security number on a withdrawal slip is not standard practice; there were red flags all over this.

We were also grateful that they accessed the account a day before Ryan's most recent paycheck, which included his annual bonus — the thief could have walked away with a lot more money.

Something like this can take months to unravel. Once I stopped feeling sorry for myself, I had other more important shit to do. First was another call to the bank to open a fraud claim.

We locked down our credit even further by alerting all our cards about the fraud. I also called the credit reporting unions to put a hold on all credit inquiries for ninety days, so no one could open a new account without me getting a phone call.

I also filed a police report, and they told me there were forty people or so going around Chicago doing this. They also weren't surprised that they somehow got my social security number — the officer shrugged and said, "These are criminals, they know what they're doing."

We closed down our accounts with that particular bank and went to a new one. We changed all our online passwords and added a verbal security password that we had to give in person at the bank to prove our identity.

I was able to turn these shitty moments into something that didn't suck so bad, and it felt good that I was able to do so. When I could have chosen to curl up in a ball on the floor, I didn't. I'm naturally trusting. Maybe it's the Canadian in me — I really do believe that most people mean to do good and the bad eggs are quite rare.

Sure, I check the locks on the door, carry a modest cross-body bag, don't have flashy things to flash, and don't leave my purse hanging on the back of a public chair — ever (my cousin had her purse stolen this way in Toronto). I take obvious precautions, and then let it go. If I obsessed or worried about every potential bad thing that could happen, I'd probably never leave the house. And I believe that whatever I focus on will be exactly what I get. For this reason, I choose to focus on the good.

I also believe that if anything is ever taken from me, then maybe I wasn't intended to have it in the first place. So holding onto it is a waste of my energy.

It took a few weeks to get the money back in our account. I like to think the universe was ready to hand me more just for trusting, for having to eat the shit sandwiches, for surrendering to the experience.

I think that whatever was taken from me will be returned tenfold in other ways.

I see you

When Jacob was getting started in hockey, we were at the rink at least three days a week. Since Talia was born, we've dragged her around to all of Jacob's events: soccer, baseball, karate, and hockey.

We didn't worry about it too much initially. It was an unavoidable complication of being the younger sibling, and she'd have her own things when she was old enough.

Out of convenience, we signed Talia up for gymnastics in the same building as Jacob's hockey.

On one particular day, I was juggling too many things. I was on a conference call for my corporate job, fumbling with Jacob's goalie pads, and getting Talia dressed and ready for gymnastics.

As soon as we arrived at the arena, she fell apart in a hangry meltdown. "I want fries and ketchup," she moaned like a starving child, even though she'd just had snacks in the car on the five-minute drive over.

"No — you start in five minutes, there's not enough time, and I don't have any cash on me," I snapped. She erupted into tears. I ignored her while I continued wrestling with smelly hockey pads and half-listening to the conference call.

She was still crying when I brought her to her gymnastics

coach. I handed her red, wet-faced little body to the instructor, explained she was just mad at me for not letting her have another snack, and made a mad dash back to finish getting Jacob ready for the ice.

Five minutes later, Jacob was skating around the rink, and I returned to the lobby and popped open my laptop to get an hour of work in with no kid interruptions. I'd peek in on the kids a few times over the hour because I liked seeing them do their thing and so they'd know I was there.

Before I even glanced at my email, the gymnastics teacher approached me, holding Talia in her arms, and handed her over like a sack of potatoes. "Hi Mom, Talia isn't participating today and is just following me around. She did this last week too. I have too many kids to watch to hold her hand during the whole class. I'm really sorry." She made a sad face, left Talia with me, and walked away.

Shit.

My gut reaction was to fire back, "Well, what the hell am I paying you for? Bring her ass back out there!" Instead, I shut up and sat Talia down beside me. I just stared at her, not sure what to do next — hoping for some divine intervention from the parenting gods telling me what to do.

I asked her why she wasn't doing gymnastics. No answer.

"Do you want to quit?" I asked.

Silence.

I asked her a few more times, and eventually, she said, "Yes. I want to do what you said." (Meaning quitting).

Keeping a poker face and without a fuss, I picked her up, took her over to the info desk, and said we were canceling because she didn't want to do gymnastics anymore. Done. I wasn't going to force her.

I sat back down with Talia, and she started whining for snacks again. "No snacking!" I told her. "You should be in gymnastics. I'm not here to play. You can go back in there, and we can play after." One of the workers then came over to me and suggested I stay in class with her. I asked Talia if this is what she wanted, and she excitedly nodded.

I closed my laptop, took her hand, and walked her out onto the gym floor. She was practically bouncing. (She was also literally bouncing because she was on a trampoline.)

Every three seconds, she looked over at me, waving excitedly. "Hi, Mommy!" She went through class, asking if I was going to watch every single activity. I said yes.

And it smacked me right in the face.

She wants me to see her. Truly see her.

She'd had enough of being carted around to her brother's activities. She had also had enough of me sitting in the lobby and working instead of watching and waving.

I was trying to do and be all the things to everyone and doing a terrible job at most of them. I felt like a huge asshat.

After a few more attempted handstands and bridges, she had to pee so I took her into the bathroom, sat her tiny body on the big toilet, and crouched down in front of her.

We locked eyes and for a moment, we were just staring at each other. I didn't have any words for her.

The words finally came. I asked her, "Does it make you sad when I'm not watching you do gymnastics?"

"Yes," she answered flatly without a hint of emotion.

Overcome with guilt, I started to cry.

Talia is an empath and cries when she sees other people crying. As her lower lip quivered, she asked, "What's wrong, Mommy?"

"I'm sorry."

"For what?"

"For not watching you in gymnastics. I'm so sorry. I'm going to watch you every time. Do you forgive me?"

"No."

With a shocked look on my face, I asked her, "What? Don't you forgive me?"

"What does forgive mean?" she asked, confused.

I chuckled. "It means that even though I did something bad, it means you can forget about it and still love me."

"Okay, I forgive you."

I hugged her sweaty little body so tight. "I'm so lucky I know you. Let's get back out there."

I can't do it all. I needed yet another reminder. This one was a smack in the face. It was time to figure out just what "having it all" meant to me anyway. What did I actually want?"

I keep needing this lesson. I'm going to show up, just fucking show up. Put the distractions away and be there.

Even if I find it boring to watch half a dozen kids picking leotard wedgies while they do somersaults and bounce around, I'm going to do it. At that moment, I had absolutely no hesitation. My job was to close my laptop and watch Talia's gymnastics class, even though it bored me to tears. Other parents don't warn you about the painfully dull moments of parenting (and there are plenty of them). I've had many moments where I invent other (almost as boring but seemingly more important) tasks just to avoid doing something like watch kids stretching or play Monopoly.

When these moments of clarity strike, we have to grasp them and hold on. All the little daily choices add up and remind us of our priorities.

Oh, yes, I will put away my phone, shut my laptop, close my book — and put both eyes directly on you.

I see you.

Slow slow slow the holidays

For so many, the holiday season means rushing around like a crazy person from one party to the next, baking cookies, decorating the house, shopping, going to holiday concerts, and getting together with all those people you promised a drink with. All the obligations — and those RumChata cocktails you're guzzling — can leave your head spinning.

What a difference from my spoiled childhood days of presents from my grandparents piled halfway up the tree.

While everyone is busy complaining that this year's Starbucks cup is not holiday-inspired enough or too red and green, I'm that jolly asshole who watches all the holiday movies and spreads cheer like a National Lampoon movie.

Christmas Eve used to be my favorite day of the year. We'd usually spend it at my vavó and vavô's house, stuffing our faces with a seafood feast, drinking too much, and going to midnight mass. Not necessarily in that order. And there was always stewed Portuguese shrimp at midnight because what else do you need after an eating marathon than a steaming pile of garlicky shrimp?

Moving away from Canada (both times) made all the holidays different. The Canadian Thanksgiving is in October, so the US one happening at the end of November never felt right. The only thing I like about Thanksgiving is pumpkin pie, so I could skip the whole thing and not be mad about it.

At Christmas, we'd either hope for great weather and travel to Canada and then have to navigate between my now-divorced parents' homes, deciding which days we'd spend where, or we'd visit Ryan's mom in Florida or his dad in upstate New York. Because Christmas is my favorite, and Ryan hates it (he's also half Jewish), I'd usually win that discussion, and we'd visit Canada. Or, sometimes, we'd stay home.

In the years we ended up staying home, I was a spoiled brat about it all. I'd listen to all the music, deck the halls, and come Christmas Eve, when I knew I was missing out on my Portuguese seafood feast, I'd turn into the scrooge of Christmas present.

And then there was the guilt. I'd feel guilty for not traveling up — especially the year my vavó died. And then I'd feel guilt for not being happy to be home, with my healthy family. Moving away from where I grew up, I had to get used to doing all the holidays somewhere else. Combine it with the kids having limited time off from school and sports, and we spent the latter half of December staring at one another.

In years when we did travel, there'd be family arguments about who was hosting or who had to bring what. I've watched more Christmases than I can count where the family wasn't speaking to each other.

When the kids were little, I felt the pressure to give them a perfect Christmas. But when they write Christmas lists to Santa in July and include three new video game consoles plus a dirt bike, I wonder, how the heck am I supposed to do it all and afford it all? And should I even try to do it? I quit.

Every year, Ryan and I would say, "screw this noise; let's go away." I'm not going to fuss about a Martha Stewart perfect anything. Besides — who said that chick was perfect? You know she went to prison, right? PRISON.

In 2019, we did it. We screwed the obligations and went to the noisiest city in the country: Las Vegas. Yes, with kids. I got a lot of strange looks from everyone when chatting casually about our holiday plans.

We told the kids that the trip was our present that year. Talia frowned and protested, "I didn't ask for that."

Fast forward to Christmas Eve hanging out in our eighteenth-floor suite overlooking the strip. It was our first full day in Vegas and, according to the kids' step-tracker, we clocked thirteen miles zigzagging through casinos to admire the holiday displays. We ate a steady diet of desserts and french fries throughout the day and finished the evening with a lovely dinner at my favorite French restaurant on the strip. Because we weren't tired enough, we caught the Bellagio fountain holiday display then headed to the roof of the Cosmopolitan for a little ice-skating in the desert.

Skating in the desert — especially for a hockey player — sucked as bad as it sounds. Three laps in, Talia hit the wall, so I took her back to the room. Jacob and Ryan would meet us when Jacob had enough of skating at a snail's pace behind the wobbly-ankled people who also thought skating in the desert would be fun.

We got back to the room, I tucked myself in to do some reading, and the boys returned. Jacob had a troubled look on his face.

I had to nudge him a few times to spill what was up.

"It doesn't feel like Christmas," he finally said.

Fuck.

I felt like this was all our fault. In an effort to change up Christmas, had we gone too far?

While we didn't miss piling presents halfway up the plastic tree filled with more plastic things that would just end up in a dumpster before our next move, we might have pushed too far with "skipping Christmas."

Instead of getting into it after the longest day in Vegas vacation history, we chatted with the kids in the morning over a Starbucks breakfast in bed. They agreed that it was the *feelings* they missed — of waking up in their beds to see what presents appeared under the tree.

Digging deeper, those feelings — not about unwrapping toys that they'll play with for twenty minutes, but the anticipation, excitement, wonder, connection — *that's* what they missed.

While the Christmas Eve meltdown was exacerbated by the strip-walking marathon and a sugar overdose, the rest of the trip was filled with more of those emotions they craved. Still exhausting, but we made it through the change. I'm not sure if we'll ever go back to Vegas for Christmas, but we will still travel when we can.

The lesson in this change was a gift.

Jingle bells aside, we seem to have forgotten what any of the holidays are all about. Since when did I have to become a Pinterest-perfect working mom with a magazine-worthy fireplace and the organic, gluten-free, nut-free, soy-free, dairy-free treats to match?

It's the company that matters. Sure, sometimes my company that Christmas in Vegas led me to sneak down to the casino to stick a fiver in a slot machine.

It's not about the perfect Instagram picture of a pristine home. It's about the conversation. It's the connection. It's all the things you didn't realize could spark joy until you put down all the armor, twinkle, and glitter, and let the '70s paneling and patchy dead grass shine on through.

After some of our early days of marriage when I made sure to follow all the rules — holiday cards with smiling family, host a party, go to all the parties, make sure everyone gets the gifts on their wish list — I decided to pull the plug on pressure.

I see people post shit on social media like "Ugh, Christmas

cards are finally done!" and wonder how special you think I'll feel when I get your unsigned card in the mail? Did you send me a card that's never even touched your hands? (*Psst*, I also saw that picture on Facebook in August.)

First, no one said you *have* to send cards. Or to every acquaintance and long-lost relative you've ever had. You have the choice to skip it. No one is going to be offended, and if they are, and they even tell you about it — they're not your people. Nope — then skip them.

If sending cards or gifts feels like a chore any time of the year — stop. If you resent every five-dollar, Hallmark-aisle purchase for birthdays and holidays, that angry energy is being infused into your card. Save it. If you still decide to send them out — do it with intention. Write a few a night. Write something personal. It takes less than a minute to write one card. Instead of sending out three hundred, send twenty. Send twenty cards to people you want to connect with, and share joy with people who help you feel good.

You can also send Valentines if December is too much. Just imagine the recipient's delight in getting a surprise card in the months following the holidays when the mail is filled with overdue bills for shit they don't remember buying.

Birthdays are also super simple now around my house. The birthday celebrator gets to choose what we eat for dinner and will get a few presents or an experience. I go buy my own presents. Spending an afternoon shopping at a bookstore alone and sipping a latte is my idea of a wild birthday.

Whatever you celebrate, spread joy like a fairy or skip the whole thing. Speaking of fairies, Talia asked me when she was seven if there was a tooth fairy. "Nope," I told her. She was a little confused, but all she really cared about was if she'd still get cash. When I assured her I'd still give her a buck for a tooth, she'd pull out a tooth, serve it up to me in her open palm, and demand her money. Sometimes the fairy doesn't need much magic.

If the mere mention of any holiday brings up a burp bubble and makes you think about the stress, the rushing, and the obligations — oh, the obligations! — then for the love of all things baby Jesus (and I love Jesus, just not the one from church), you could change how you do the holidays.

Belonging nowhere and nowhere

Maya Angelou said, "You only are free when you realize you belong no place — you belong every place — no place at all."

When it comes to belonging with people, family always feels like belonging. And having lived in two countries and five states, I've learned that discovering a sense of belonging with new people always takes a while too. That knowledge weighs on me immediately following the decision to move. *But our friends, and our network* — it always feels like a pull keeping us from moving forward, even when we know a move is necessary for growth or change.

Ryan and I have lived far away from family for most of our married lives, and every time we move, it feels as if we're breaking into a secret club. Making friends as an adult can feel awkward — *hey, new human, can I, like, text you sometime?* After spending five years in our last home in Illinois, saying goodbye to our friends was hard.

"We'll come visit!" they say, and every now and again someone will follow through, but people are busy, especially those with kids, jobs, and friends (so, most people). And every time we move, we start again with just the four of us.

Having stayed in the same school with the same small group

of friends from kindergarten through sixth grade, I appreciated having history with some of my friends, and this is something that Jacob and Talia won't know because we've moved so much.

In any home we've owned that had a front porch, you'd find me out there. It's my way of feeling connected to the outside world. When a neighbor comes outside, I try to look busy, like I'm not trying to intrude on them, but at the same time silently convey, "Hey, hi, I'm here. Want to talk?" That's what I want to say, but never do.

"We should get together sometime," they sometimes say.

I nod. "Yup, definitely."

What I really want to say is, "How about tonight? I'm free tomorrow too." I am so available because I didn't grow up here and have no family obligations, birthday parties, and real-life local friends. While having the opportunity to live in many different places is fun at times, it can also leave me feeling terribly lonely.

The duality of belonging and not belonging feels true in our home too. We belong all over our house, and we also don't feel like we belong there all the time, especially when it's overrun with people and stuff.

When you live amongst clutter and an abundance of stuff, especially if it's someone else's stuff, it can feel like a sumo wrestler is sitting on your chest. Like wearing an itchy sweater when you're craving something soft, like an old sweatshirt. But how do you even ask for or create your own space? Isn't that selfish?

I grew up in a small family, but I remember there was always *someone* home — someone in my space. Someone in the common area I was enjoying. When Ryan and I married and later welcomed Jacob and Talia, that feeling crept in again. My space wasn't mine anymore. It was full of someone else's crap: Legos, toys, dolls, socks, and snotty tissues. And smells too — *whose aroma is this?*

In the early days of motherhood, when Ryan would get

home from work, I'd often disappear and lock myself in the bathroom for a little longer than someone should take in the bathroom. Especially on the weekend when I just wanted some quiet — I wanted time to be alone. To sit, to think, to simply be still and silent. Without someone talking to me. Without anyone demanding my time or my attention.

I craved more time to be alone with my thoughts. I needed my own space. Even when I was a kid, I was delighted to find myself home alone, and now as an adult and a parent, it feels like pure, peaceful bliss. I recognize the conflict of feeling both lonely and wanting to be alone. Where do I belong?

This is why I think we carve out our favorite spot on the couch and claim it as our own. I can sit and write comfortably if I'm on the left side of the sofa, but if I'm on the right side or the loveseat, I feel off — like when one sock slides down your foot inside your boot.

When I'd work from home for my corporate job, I'd set up shop on the couch. Until I realized we had an entire office to use in our south Chicago home. I decided that was going to be *my* room. I added a ton of my art to the walls, cleaned it from top to bottom, and claimed it as my personal space.

When I have my own personal retreat space in my home or even when traveling, that space is sacred. It's just for me. By physically retreating from a common area with all the other breathing souls to a little nook in my home that feels like it's truly my own, I get more space to think. It makes creation — writing — feel more natural and more effortless.

It's even better if that space has a door. Bonus points if the door has a lock on it. In our last home, my office could only lock from the outside. So if I ever got locked in, I'd have all the space in the world — except I wouldn't be able to eat or go to the bathroom. But I wouldn't be able to do laundry or cook dinner either. Maybe that's okay too.

I have a few little spaces of my own that feel like me. My side of the bed, where I have a stack of books, some pens and journals, and a yoga mat. It's my little space where my introverted self can retreat and go within when the outer noise gets too loud. I belong with my family, and I belong alone.

In our demanding world of people calling the shots for our time and energy, when I intentionally create space for myself, it's a massive act of self-care.

I stock my spaces with things that bring a smile to my face. Today, this looks like lung-healthy soy candles, citrine, quartz, amethyst, butterfly wings in little jars, oracle cards, notebooks that feel good to write in, and pens that feel good to wield.

Open space, whether that's a blank calendar or my physical environment, can feel scary, like starting with a blank page or an empty canvas. But when I allow myself to show up and be me, it can feel wildly freeing. I have freedom to choose where I belong.

I belong to myself. Wherever I am, there I am. As long as I'm home in myself, I'm at home in the world.

V. GOING ALL-IN ON ME

"Besides, no one's interested in something you didn't do."

Tragically Hip, "Wheat Kings"

We are here for a purpose. Some of us find it in our work, some find it at home, some find it in our play. It took me eight years to go from "Hmm, I could do work I actually like and get paid," to going all-in on me. It took eight years, and it took commitment. Over and over, I recommitted to myself, my craft, my family. Our life's work comprises many of our waking thoughts and energy. Only when I stepped into work that felt really good for me did it start to change my entire life.

Dismissed

With my marketing degree in hand, I did what any reasonable twenty-one-year-old does — I took the first job I could find. I landed a great job at the headquarters for a retail chain in Canada and did the corporate climb for several months before I left the country to marry Ryan.

Once I got that long-awaited US work permit, I again took the first well-paying job I could. It was management consulting, which had nothing to do with marketing, but I said yes to everything, pulled up my Spanx, and climbed another corporate ladder.

And damn was I good at navigating that ladder. As a management consultant and then in corporate communications, the word "creative" was never part of my vocabulary. Creativity didn't belong in my professional world — that was for other people. I wore dress pants and heels — I was fancy.

I completely identified with my job — I was important.

One day, sitting in my shiny new Chicago office, I got an email from HR. My temporary work visa was expiring, and unless I could show my new one, I wouldn't be allowed to work there. It was expiring *the next day*. I'm mostly on top of my shit, and I knew it was expiring. I was awaiting my green card and had been following up with the appropriate agencies. But the work visa had somehow fallen through the cracks while I was focused on the green card, which would have made the work visa unnecessary.

We were on my health insurance. I couldn't just stop working tomorrow. My managing director was copied on that email and, soon after, he poked his head over my cube with a face that read, *what the fuck?* Tears in my eyes and feeling full of shame, I explained the whole situation and promised I would figure it out.

I had no idea what to do. I called Ryan and, smart cookie that he is, he had a suggestion: Visit the local US immigration office ASAP and demand my work permit get renewed. *Can I really do that? Doesn't the agency get to tell me what to do? I have to play by their rules.*

Hardly sleeping that night, playing out all the different scenarios in my head, I took the early train to the downtown Chicago immigration office. I was first in line before the doors opened. The security guard opened the doors as the line stretched around the corner, hopeful people queued up with manila folders in hand. I was one of them.

The guard asked if I had an appointment. I didn't. I quickly explained, pleading my case. He let me in, I saw someone right away, and was granted an extension on my work permit. I went back to the office, scanned my new work permit, sent it to HR, and got back to work. That was a close call. My green card showed up a month later.

I completely appreciate how fortunate I was to have been able to get this straightened out so quickly. And for all the times I left the immigration office frustrated and feeling stupid, this time, I was grateful.

I went back to that shiny ladder climbing without missing a rung.

When I was pregnant with Jacob, I continued proving my worth. I set out to show everyone (not that anyone asked me to) that I'd be able to do more than all my colleagues while pregnant. Well, that pressure I put on myself resulted in many nights working until midnight and feeling like crap.

A few months back to work after having Jacob, work just felt so — meaningless. Everything felt pointless, and I started to resent the meetings, the endless and sometimes unreasonable flow of demands, and wondered if there was something else. I didn't know what I wanted, but I had a feeling that this was *not it*.

I was working with a Chicago management consulting company and mostly worked on huge government projects. Right after President Obama took his seat in office in 2009, government budgets for some contractors were cut.

We lost some big projects, and we weren't busy — which is terrible news for any business. I had no idea what to expect when my managing director called me into his office one Monday afternoon, where I sat down with some dude from HR who I'd never met. It took me a minute to realize what was happening. Then I noticed the look on my boss's face. I was getting shit-canned, and I wasn't the only one. Our discussion was purposefully quick. Budgets, losing projects, margins weren't where they needed to be, and so on.

They let me take my time to gather my things quietly and leave the building with dignity.

My laptop bag stuffed with the contents of my desk and everything but my laptop, I didn't make eye contact with anyone on the way out. I rode the train home that day totally numb. *I've worked my entire life, who am I without work?* I held my shit together until I got home. When I walked up the flight of steps, punched in our door code, and stepped into our condo, finally, I cried. I cried an ugly cry only someone who has no idea what they are going to do with their life cries. In addition to not knowing what I was going to do with my life, there was the stress of being a new mom, having a mortgage in the middle of the 2009 crash, and being a significant financial contributor to the household. I felt like such a loser.

In the days that followed, I mostly cried a lot and fought with Ryan. When I realized this was unproductive, I shifted into get-shit-done mode and contacted everyone I knew. I also tried to enjoy the unexpected extra time with Jacob — a bonus maternity leave. Besides, it was summer, so I'd spend mornings and evenings looking for jobs and conducting interviews (which were few and far between) and spend afternoons at the beach with my little boy.

I've always provided for myself (except for that six months after immigrating and waiting for my work visa), so the hardest part was relying on Ryan financially. I also missed the adult interaction outside of mommy groups. I missed being a contributing member of society.

On top of this, I was navigating these feelings during a recession and a crash in the housing market. We had to execute a short sale on a lousy property purchase, which would take us the next decade to finally pay off. I had to apply for unemployment. I had to learn not to feel embarrassed about any of it.

At this time, we'd been toying with the idea of moving to Toronto so that we could be closer to my family. Jacob was a year old, so having some help would be a blessing. Also, we really wanted the kids to grow up knowing their grandparents. My vavó was still alive too, so they'd get to know their great grandmother.

I started looking for a job in Toronto rather than Chicago. It happened at record speed; I landed a RIM-job — they used to go by the name Research In Motion, now BlackBerry. This was when BlackBerry was doing exceptionally well — private employee concerts with U2 and Def Leppard kind of well. I landed an awesome gig in crisis communications, and they paid to relocate all three of us. It was Ryan's turn to immigrate now from the United States to Canada, which was definitely easier than my move to the US. Ryan could (and did) work right away.

I did my thing, climbing the climb, learning tons about BlackBerry technical infrastructure — stuff you can't learn in school. A year or so into the job though, that little nagging knowing at the back of my mind told me I wasn't happy there. It was a great job, and they treated me well; it just felt — off.

This was when I discovered self-development books and was reading all kinds of books with the same message — you can do work you love and get paid for it!

What do you mean? Work is supposed to suck. You mean, I could do something different like even create my own business?

I spent many nights on the couch, dreaming up business ideas. I could sell bean burger recipes! I had a long list of ideas and eventually decided to start a blog about plant-based food. We had just gone vegan after all, so I had lots to write about and was creating a ton of new recipes. I'd start a blog, maybe make some money, and figure out how to turn it into a business from there. For now, I had no intention of quitting my day job; I'd enjoy the creative outlet and regular paychecks.

They were killing it when I joined, but a few years later when the iPhone gained popularity and BlackBerry didn't keep up, we started to shrink. Layoffs there came in waves. I'd hear about them on the news in the morning and drive to work wondering if that day would be my last. Since BlackBerry is a high-profile company, there were news trucks outside whenever layoffs were happening. After each round of layoffs, we would get company-wide emails letting us know which business functions were no longer necessary and reassuring anyone reading that our jobs were safe — for now.

Ryan had an opportunity at a start-up back in Chicago (the job came with a start-up salary: read, less money) and was traveling back and forth to test it out. We were considering a move, and with BlackBerry's instability, we figured I'd stick it out there as long as I could.

News of another round of layoffs hit the press, so we all knew we were on the chopping block. My gut told me that morning my number was up, so I was prepared with a backup phone and my personal laptop in my car. I said to my team as I set down my vanilla soy latte, "If we get shit-canned today, meet me at Starbucks later." Sadly, a bunch of them met me there a few hours later.

When a director approached our quad of desks and called two of us to follow him, I knew it was happening. My knowing was confirmed when we landed in a conference room, and I laid eyes on a stack of manila envelopes in the center of the table. The coworker I was with started to cry while I was stone-faced. The first thing out of my mouth: "How much is severance, and when will I get it?"

This time, we were escorted out by security. There wasn't an opportunity to go back to my desk to collect my belongings — they'd pack and ship me my stuff. They only asked if I needed anything from my cube before I left. I'm not sure if that left me with more or less dignity than my first layoff experience.

As we approached the security door, my manager started apologizing to me. Dismissively, I apologized to him instead — I told him I couldn't imagine being in his position that day. He lowered his head and said, "This is the worst day of my career."

I worked at BlackBerry for three years, minus a maternity leave when I had Talia. This layoff was the trigger to put the rest of our plan B in motion. Right away, I applied for unemployment benefits and emailed my old boss from Chicago on a whim to see what was new, telling him we were planning to move back to Chicago. This was the management consulting company that laid me off in 2009.

He called me later that afternoon. "We just won some massive government contracts, when can you come back?" The work was part of the rollout of Obamacare, and they hired back almost everyone from my old team.

"Um… give me a month?" We sold our new-construction home for a tidy profit, found a rental in Chicago, hired a fantastic nanny, and executed an international move in four weeks with two kids (then one and four) and two dogs. We don't mess around.

At first, it was a little weird being back at the place that handed me my first pink slip in 2009. Now, in 2012, with my old team back together, it felt like the old days. Life was good.

Having been let go twice now, I knew this was not my forever job. The excitement of new projects with old colleagues quickly wore off, and I shifted my focus to establishing and growing my own business on the side. I had maintained my plant-based food blog and was teaching local cooking classes now, doing food demos, and crafting meal plans for busy professionals who wanted to eat more vegetables but didn't have time to cook. It was a nice little side-hustle, and it was a lot of fun.

In the year I was back at my old company, I racked up a few pay raises and two promotions. I quickly proved how much I had learned while I was gone. I'd had another baby, moved twice, and had some handy new communications skills under my belt now.

That voice asking if this was all there was crept back up again. The whisper would quiet whenever I was in the midst of a big transition, like moving or having babies, but it never really went away. I knew my days were numbered again when some contracts expired, and there weren't any new ones coming in. I was proactively looking for another job this time. My side business wasn't at the point that I could quit my corporate job and quickly grow it to replace my income. Our family relied on my paycheck, and it was too big a risk for me to simply stop working.

Following a taco Tuesday lunch, I received a 2:10 p.m. meeting invitation (layoffs are almost always on a Monday or Tuesday) from a managing director I hardly spoke with. The meeting was scheduled in a conference room, not her corner office. When I arrived and saw their somber faces, I didn't even try to contain my laughter. Before they even had a chance to speak, I cut them off. Gesturing to the papers in the center of the table, I said, "I know the drill. How much is severance?"

Eyes wide, they looked at me like I was crazy.

Bye!

On my walk home, I stopped at the grocery store, bought a twenty-five-dollar bottle of wine, some good chocolate, and flowers. I actually skipped back home — I was free.

No one is layoff proof

Here are the essential lessons from being laid off three times in five years (twice from the same company).

Crying is unproductive, so do what you need to do to unlock get-shit-done mode and contact everyone you know. This is why staying in touch with people and networking *before* you need to is always a good idea.

Apply for unemployment insurance right away. It feels incredibly vulnerable, I get it. I did it three times and I didn't die. You pay for it so please don't feel weird about it, just do it. If you can, try to enjoy the time — especially if you have severance pay. Time is our most valuable currency anyway.

Look for another job immediately. Even if you have four months of severance pay, that's roughly how long it took me to go from pink slip to new employee orientation all three times. And for us, sometimes it made sense to go into some debt. I know this isn't for everyone, but for us, it was a leap of faith.

Before it happens, start a side-hustle. If you get your pink slip, your side-hustle could become your full-time income, or it could help you build your savings account and save your ass when the time comes. At the very least, you'll have a creative outlet. This way, if you find yourself jobless, you can have enough momentum going on the side that you can quickly sweep in and shift your focus while keeping your bank account healthy.

Trust that the layoff is not personal. In significant layoffs, it comes down to a percentage point on a spreadsheet. Even though I felt like the biggest loser in the world, I had some candid conversations about my personal numbers on the spreadsheet. You really are just a number sometimes — even if a company *says* they're people first, they are a business first, and the health of the business sometimes means reorganizing.

No one is layoff-proof. You can be extremely valuable and well-liked, but sometimes it all comes down to numbers. The old-school dream of getting a job and working there until you die is dead. Prepare yourself for a layoff and make a plan that includes household budgets, both pre- and post-layoff. Outline what subscriptions and services you'll cancel the moment the "trigger" is pulled. This also means your LinkedIn profile and résumé should always be ready.

On a similar note, there's no such thing as job security. When people say their job offers them "stability," I cringe. It provides you a routine and a paycheck — until it doesn't. In a regular nine-to-five, you have the illusion of predictability and security, but often very little, if any, control.

Your job is not you. When we use a job, title, or role to define us, the blow hurts when we lose it. If you're not identifying yourself and basing your self-worth on your career and how many Spanx you own, you won't feel like a piece of you is lost when you lose your job.

Layoffs happen for a reason. It's the universe's way of offering you a better opportunity — and maybe giving you a severance package while you figure it out. In my case, the universe had cranked up the volume to eleven, turned on the flashing neon lights, and pulled not only the rug from under my feet but the foundation too.

I ignored those nudges the first two times, and after the third, I knew it was time to do something different. I was going to go all-in on me. It was game on.

Screw your well-roundedness

I used to try to be good at everything — a Jacq of all trades. Even in my first job as a cashier, I bounced from stocking auto parts, watering plants, and organizing the bowling league. See where that got me? Three layoffs in five years taught me that there's no such thing as job security. I had a choice — go into victim mode or action mode. After the third layoff, I told myself that I never wanted to be fired again. The next time, I'd be in control.

When that final layoff happened, sure, I skipped home and celebrated with wine and chocolate, but I still needed to find another job. My side-hustle was thriving, but it wasn't enough to cover the financial bases. We were two weeks away from closing on a new home, and they hadn't done the employment verification yet. If they waited past the date of my two weeks' notice, they'd discover I didn't have a job, and we wouldn't get the house. I kept calm. I can't explain it, but I *knew* that everything would work out. I trusted that we'd be okay.

I did some finagling and was able to bump our closing up and, lucky me, because I didn't have a job, I had plenty of time to orchestrate a move. This one was only thirty miles south of Chicago.

As luck would have it, I told the listing agent who was selling our condo rental that I was looking for a job. He said his fiancée worked at a great consulting company, one that touted no unwanted travel — travel being the bane of a consultant's existence when the excitement of all those air miles and points dry up. He gave me her contact info, I emailed her that afternoon, and she sent in a referral for me. A few months later, I had a shiny new management consulting job.

I was a different person going into this role and vowed I'd take a different attitude toward my work. This job turned out to be the most fun of all the jobs I've worked. I had plenty of creative freedom, and I ran a lot of communications initiatives. Around this time, I had quit being vegan, so the food blog lost its luster. This was when it clicked — writing the blog was the thing I liked best about food blogging.

It was a huge a-ha moment. I was writing more than ever, creating communication plans and writing emails that people would want to open. The goal of many of those emails was to get employees to take action, to learn a new tool, to do things a new way. It was persuasive writing at its finest.

My colleagues would ask me if I could help them with their LinkedIn profiles, write proposals, spiff up PowerPoints with great (and super simple) copy. I had finally discovered my sweet spot. And only eight years after I sensed that I could do so much more.

About a year into that job, I started my freelance copywriting business. My goal at the time was to grow it until it provided enough regular income that I could justify leaving the corporate world and making something happen on my own.

With one foot out the door, I was still extremely grateful to my corporate job. Since I did a lot of writing, I had daily opportunities to hone my skills, especially communication.

During my last corporate performance review, I told my manager I wanted to continue working on my writing, to make it stronger and try out new ways of communicating at our company. And he told me about three new-to-me software systems I needed to learn. You know, because I needed to be more "well-rounded."

I wanted to double-down on all my communication skills and go from good to great. "I don't want to improve my weaknesses, I want to work on my strengths instead."

This is what I said to my then-manager — which turned out to be the performance review that helped push me out the corporate door for the last time.

Since our school-age days, the most well-intentioned teachers tell us that we should focus on our weaknesses and work to turn them into strengths. But when we're busy focusing on weaknesses, we lose sight of what we're naturally great at.

If your weaknesses don't serve you, consider this — maybe ignore them and see if you can work with people who are strong in your weak spots.

Also, why are we so adamant about pointing out our weaknesses and the weaknesses of others? So what? Let's spend more time noticing the stuff we're good at so we can keep pushing and working on getting better at that.

Of course, you'll have interests outside of your zone of genius, too, and that's totally okay. Work on things that light you up and make you buzz with enthusiasm.

How do you know when you're working in your zone of genius? What strengths should you focus on? If you're not sure — do some digging — ask your friends, family, and coworkers some things they think you excel at. Make a list of all the things people are always asking for your advice on. Even if the topics are diverse, look for the themes.

When you're doing those things, how does it feel? Do you get lost in time and could do what you're doing for hours? When you're not doing this stuff, do you wish you were?

I completely ignored my manager's advice, didn't even log in to the new software I was supposed to learn, and kept on writing because I believe that what you focus on expands. Writing was fun and creative. I enjoyed it while doing it, and I loved seeing the impact it had — to make a sale, to get someone a job, or to create a change. Words have so much power, and I loved slinging them, playing with them, and shaping them into something beautiful.

There have been many times I've sat across from a manager or a boss who held the keys to a promotion, more money, or access to good projects, and they've said things to me like, "You need to diversify," or "Picking up this skill would make you more well-rounded," and "You can't focus on just these few skills."

Here, hold my wine.

You'd never ask my software architect husband to learn how to write speeches for the CEO, balance a ledger, or order lunch for the team. Why are we asking creatives to "expand"? What if we're expanding when we sit down to work on what we do best? What if we're supposed to follow those nudges — pick up a paintbrush, grab a scrapbook, or open a blank page?

If we don't focus on getting really good at a few things, we'll spend our lives dabbling on the surface level of a bunch of shit, and never going deep.

When someone asks you to work on skills at the opposite end of your strengths, question their intention. When someone says you "should" do work that dulls your shine and makes you want to throw up while tweezing your eyelashes, get curious about your reaction.

This isn't about shying away from a challenge or stretching your skills — it's about staying clear on the ones that light you up and will serve your work.

After spending too many years awkwardly trying to get good at things I didn't care about, I said, "Screw this!"

Instead of focusing on my weaknesses, I now only concentrate on my strengths.

Because I said *no* to learning tech, becoming an Excel wiz, getting a project manager certification, or becoming more "well-rounded," I had time to grow my copywriting skills, spiff up my ruthless editing talents, and help others with their writing.

Writing and coaching are my jam. Especially when it comes to making something fussy sound simple or something boring sound fun — making things that no one wants to read, readable. Helping people create a new writing habit, helping people feel less shitty about their writing — that's what lights my fire.

When you pick up a heavier dumbbell and work your already muscular bicep — you get a stronger bicep.

Creating a life
I don't need a vacation from

My corporate salary was a significant portion of our household income, and I wasn't ready to eat cat food so that I could cut out my commute time and do work I loved. Ryan told me that if I could earn half of my corporate income in my side-hustle while still employed, then that would prove to be enough. We assumed that if I could earn half of my corporate dollars with freelance writing work, I'd be able to make the switch and do my work full-time — and earn a living.

I put my target quit date on the calendar six months in advance. I drafted my resignation email several times and updated the date. When work felt frustrating, and all I wanted was to sit in my home office and do my work, I popped open that email resignation that sat in my draft folder. Sometimes I'd make some slight edits, but mostly I looked at it and felt the excitement as if I were about to hit send. I'd get out of bed in the morning for months pretending that I was getting dressed to sit down to write in my home office.

I explained to Jacob and Talia that for the next few months, mommy would be really busy with work. I told them it might seem like I'm working all the time — and really, I was. I was doing all that extra work so that I could be around more later. I hope they understand someday, or that I'll make it up to them in the coming years. Maybe they've forgotten by now.

I told them I'd be able to get them from school at the end of the school day. I wouldn't need to drop them off at 6:30 a.m. anymore so I could catch the early train. I'd come on field trips, and we'd eat breakfast at home, in the kitchen — and not out of a plastic container balanced on our laps in the car.

I used every bit of extra time with intention. If I took the train to work, I'd read books about entrepreneurship or would write my website copy. During car commutes and road trips, I'd listen to audiobooks about starting, marketing, and growing an online business. If I had time between meetings or during my lunch break, I'd do some research, take online courses, or do some online networking. Every second had to count.

I'd plan out my week on Sundays and block time on my calendar to focus on business-building activities. Some days that just meant thirty minutes, and other days I wouldn't be able to focus on my business at all. But only thirty minutes a day, while I sipped my morning coffee while reading an inspirational business book, added up over the weeks and months.

I was doing all this on top of my regular job and running a household. When I buckled down and got serious, I worked no more than forty hours a week at my day job, turned down lots of invitations, worked in my business to get clients, create blog content, and write website copy — all in the mornings, evenings, and any crack of time I could find. I kept my weekends mostly free to rest my brain. Rest is important, and pushing harder would have felt crappy.

I wanted to help more people with their writing to support my growing business, so I reached out to some of my friends and former colleagues with an offer. I told them I'd give them a few hours of my time to write or edit anything they'd like in return for some candid feedback and a testimonial.

A few people took a chance on me, and I was able to give them words they could share with the world. A LinkedIn blog post that made magazines pick up the phone, bios that made photographers confident to share their website, proposals that made clients say, "hell yes!", and even a job description that got someone a sweet-ass promotion.

I was on to something. I told a few more friends, threw a price list on my website, and carried on. I didn't pay for any advertising or pimp my services to everyone I knew in a sleazy way, and something magical happened — people found me and hired me. Every evening, I'd write and edit my ass off for my new clients. I received rave reviews and they'd pass my name along to someone else, and someone else, and someone else. Before I knew it, I had so much extra work in addition to my day job that I had to start turning some new opportunities down.

In my case, I was fortunate to spend time in my day job writing internal communications and doing change management consulting. This meant I logged tens of thousands of hours working directly with clients and writing — the skills I'd need plenty of in my freelance copywriting business.

While at times, it was tempting to grumble about a crappy project, jerk boss, drama-ridden coworkers, or the never-ending flow of emails — I didn't. If I put negative energy into my day job, it could spill over into my growing business. I practiced relentless optimism. I looked at every opportunity as a chance to practice a new skill or interact with a new kind of person. Those challenging coworkers are practice for dealing with contractors. That douchey boss is practice for dealing with less than remarkable clients. That ten-page report, million-dollar proposal, or sensitive email are all chances to flex my persuasive writing skills. And, at the very least, I was always thankful for my full-time job for providing me with a steady and predictable paycheck that was helping fund my dream.

If you're exhausted reading this, know that I hit the wall many times. As much as I like to play superwoman, I am not one. I learned there was only so much pushing I could do. As a wife and working mom with kids in demanding sports, I had many moments where I considered giving up on work completely. Sometimes, having a regular job would feel more comfortable. But that came with a price. While it was the easy option to choose in the moment, that option was slowly wearing down my soul. Especially with getting laid off — the hiring, climbing, firing cycle was getting old.

When you have a full-time job and commit to working a side-hustle, it's smart to ward off burnout before it even has an opportunity to creep up when you're busy clearing your inbox. I've been there. I've experienced burnout while just having a nine-to-five. It looks like insomnia, not being able to think clearly, and blowing up on people you love and care about.

You can't pour from an empty cup, and you'll put both your day job and your side-hustle at risk if you're not careful.

Schedule a day or two a week to do nothing. Yes, literally, plan nothing work-related. Unplug, have fun, stare at the sky, and watch some cloud shapes float by. If you typically work on your side-hustle in the evening, take some time to recharge first. Eat dinner with your family, go to the gym, watch some Netflix, read a few pages of a juicy book, take a nap, then get back to your hustle with renewed vigor.

My goal was to leave by June of 2017. I did it three months sooner, in March, when they wanted to put me on a project that would require ninety miles of driving a day. The change suddenly became urgent.

But I was ready. It took roughly a year and a half to get there, but for the three consecutive months before I quit, I did it — I earned half of my corporate salary with my side-hustle. It was time to plan my exit from the nine-to-five.

It was time to create a life I looked forward to living and especially one I didn't need a vacation from.

I quit!

With sweaty palms and my stomach doing backflips, I scheduled a call with my manager. I had been fired three times in my career, but quitting was something I had never done. *Do I send him an email? A text message? A meeting request?* I asked Ryan for advice, figuring he would know — this was a man, after all, who once had eight different jobs in a single year. That's a story for another day.

I emailed my manager to tell him I'd call him the next morning. I made the call in the car on my drive in; after some awkward small talk, I got right to it. My manager understood and truly wished me well. As soon as I hung up, I turned onto Lakeshore Drive, admiring Lake Michigan, and started laughing uncontrollably. Now I really felt free. Free to choose every bit of work I focus on. It was such a huge relief.

This total journey time from "I think I want to do something different with my life" to "I quit" was eight years. It took me almost a decade to kinda sorta figure out what I wanted to do with my life. There were many times when I'd lose focus and slip back into Facebook scrolling on the couch, but the point is to commit again — and again, and again. It can take time.

Maybe your journey takes much longer, or you make it happen much faster. However long it takes, your timing is perfect.

I also have to acknowledge I couldn't have done this without Ryan's support. Without him having faith in me, pushing me, and also holding up the other end of the household with his income, I'm not sure I would have ever taken this risk.

On my last day I went out for tacos with my favorite colleagues, indulged in a lunch-time margarita, and then rode the elevator down the fifty-three floors for the last time.

The first few days at home were amazing. I had so much time. I could prepare a hot lunch every single day. No more meeting requests pinging me all day.

Even when, during week one of being a full-time CEO, two of my clients had to pause working with me, I didn't hesitate for a second. I doubled down on delivering for the clients I did have and spent the extra time reaching out to my old network, friends, family, and doing what I could to get visible online. For me, this meant showing up and being awesome inside of Facebook groups, connecting with other business owners in my industry and in complementary industries. I wasn't in there screaming, "Look at me! Hire me!" Gross! Instead, I looked for opportunities where I could be useful.

People asked me if I was worried about failing. And to me, it wasn't an option. There was no plan B, there was no job I'd go back to, and I knew that I'd go on to replace and then surpass my corporate income. It was nonnegotiable.

Stepping into full responsibility for me running and growing my business was an exercise in feeling the doubt and doing it anyway.

That doubt doesn't completely go away, the voice just gets quieter, and I'm more used to taking action now than in those days of dreaming about some elusive business I'd someday maybe start in the future.

I'm proud to tell you that I replaced my corporate income in a little over a year. And the best part isn't even that I did it while working twenty to thirty hours a week, with no commute. It's that I work with people I love to work with. Clients send me presents in the mail. I get cards and flowers — all for doing something fun that I enjoy. And I send just as many gifts to them. In only a few years, I have shoeboxes full of handwritten notes of gratitude.

Work that feels good and makes an impact — thank you, more please.

Slow the fuck down

I wish I could tell you all this rushing around with days filled to the brim ended when I stepped away from my corporate career to be my own boss. Even though I've limited my work to thirty hours a week, sometimes those hours crept in at the worst of times. And, occasionally, I'll take on a new project that requires more attention than I planned.

In my nine-to-five, I'd walk around like I had my shit together. The truth is that no one has all their shit together. I was showing up all done up and acting like I had everything together, when really I had just lost my shit on the kids in the car fifteen minutes earlier. They'd be fighting, and I'd scream at them. Sometimes I'd scream so loud I'd scare them. Often I had frightened myself. I felt depleted every single time. This was not the kind of mom I wanted my kids to have.

I wasn't even the kind of human I wanted to be. I hardly recognized myself.

There were seasons in my life when I had to stuff my calendar — like launching a new business while maintaining a full-time job. This pace isn't sustainable long term, so knowing there was a light at the end of the tunnel made it worth it.

And sure, there are also plenty of times when everything

comes to a screeching halt — I get sick, a kid gets sick, or I have nothing left to give.

I had to slow down and look around, be in my life, stop checking email at every stoplight because that's all the time I had.

When I cleared the headspace, lived with less stuff and fewer obligations, I could finally take the time to look at the faces of the people in my family, and give them an actual hug.

Slow the fuck down.

Maybe you've screeched this at someone on the highway and given them the one-finger salute.

I used to spend many of my waking hours with my family running around like a crazy person trying to do all the things. And regrettably, about as many yelling at the bumpers of those other cars on the highway during my commute.

I didn't have a near-death experience (thankfully); I just got sick of constantly rushing around and for what? For no reason at all.

I was rushing around for a job I hated and enduring a sucky commute, only to work with people I didn't enjoy. (Some of them, anyway; most of my coworkers were awesome.)

There's no such thing as having it all, as we're now finally learning. There are trade-offs. Reality is, I was trying to be so many things to so many people, it was hard to be really good at any of them. Something is always getting more attention, leaving something else unattended.

This looks like me getting new writing clients — while Ryan sits beside me on the couch staring at the TV, waiting for me to close my laptop. I pretend not to see him because I want to really impress this potential client with a kickass proposal. After an hour, he gives up, launches himself off the couch, and announces he's going to bed.

I had spent so many evenings sitting on the couch, tweaking my website, social media-ing, and writing, that most of my pants decided amongst themselves to shrink — how dare they!

This must be why so many business owners talk about wearing yoga pants or joining the no pants club.

I've chaperoned fewer field trips than I'm proud to admit. I barely have the patience for my own kids, so how could I muster up enough to watch, let alone enjoy, someone else's when I have so much to do? I went on a few, and when the teacher handed me all six boys in the classroom, plus a baggie with one of the kids' ADHD meds, I knew I was terribly unqualified to medicate, let alone supervise other kids. I handed that kid and his meds back to the teacher and said, "I'm not comfortable with this." That was my last field trip.

Some nights I wouldn't spend any time at all with my kids because I was so obsessed with making sure they ate healthily, took all their immunity-boosting vitamins, and got to bed on time. And then there was me packing school lunches and getting ready for the next day.

I've often wondered if we could just go back to the 1950s — when I wouldn't be expected to work. I'd just have to focus on keeping my home clean, my family fed, and myself presentable. Would I feel freer if this were the case? When do I get to lay on the couch and do nothing? Maybe I'd *feel* freer but in truth, I'd be more dependent. That's the hard truth.

The expectations of today's moms are out of control. I have to be the mom from the '50s through to 2021. I have to be all things to everyone. It's like there's a huge line of people with their hands out waiting for me to give them a piece of myself.

At the end of the day, and that was the only time when I'd have a minute to myself, I'd have nothing left for Ryan and the kids, let alone myself.

Running on empty, I'd pour a glass of wine and start scrolling through Facebook, then Instagram, and maybe Pinterest. Refreshing after several minutes because I'd been scrolling for so long — there might be something new to read. Something new to distract me from feeling empty. This overflowing life filled with obligations but very little meaning.

Going to bed with nothing left for me. I'd be too tired to give myself anything anyway. I'd just go to sleep. Besides, I had to get up at five a.m. the next day and do it all over again.

When I was putting the finishing edits on my first mini-book, *Unfussy Mom* — a book for working moms, I came pretty close to abandoning the whole project. I started wondering if both parents working was detrimental to families.

I actually like work. I need work. I think we were designed to do deep work on things that mean something to us. I also like making money. When I contribute financially to our household, we're able to live the lifestyle we want — one where we can take modest vacations and spend ungodly amounts of money on gymnastics, dance, and travel hockey.

While we could certainly scale back and start eating cereal for dinner, I don't think there's a need to compromise. And if I were to find myself without Ryan someday, I'd be able to support Jacob and Talia. I never wanted to be the kind of wife that needed to rely on her husband and had a taste of that when I was waiting for my US work permit.

Many evenings, frustrated by all the things still on my to-do list, I'd throw my arms up and declare, "That's it, I'm quitting my job! I quit everything!"

When Ryan would come home and be less than thrilled about what was for dinner, I'd snap, "Well, I have a fucking job to do, you know."

When the kids asked why I can't volunteer for their class party, I used to snap, "Mommy works," but really, I didn't want to. Those parties are booger fests and leave introverted me completely drained. I need to sleep for three days after a class party.

The kids don't give a shit if I work or not. So the example I was setting for my kids was mommy needs to work, runs around the house like crazy, makes our food, and doesn't have time to play with us, talk to us, or read us books before bed.

Could I do both? Could I work *and* read books before bed?

When I made those empty threats about quitting my day job, I knew it wouldn't happen, mainly because we had designed a lifestyle that requires a dual income. This isn't necessarily bad, and we couldn't just unwind it all overnight.

It required me to take a hard look at what was important to me. I came back to memento mori. At the end of my life, do I want to look back and feel proud of how many home-cooked meals I put together? The number of parties we attended? Or how many minutes I was face-to-face with my family?

Not my circus, not my monkeys

I'm careful about who I share my dreams with. I only told a handful of people who I knew would believe in me that I had a business idea that could replace my corporate job. It wasn't that I didn't want to tell too many people in case I failed, it was that I didn't want to share it with the haters and naysayers. I prefer to share with people who will encourage, push, and poke me with questions. What I needed were cheerleaders to lift me up.

I'd identify the people who didn't have my back pretty quickly. When I told them, "I'm working on building my freelance writing business so I can quit my job," some people laughed, some said, "good luck," and some joked about how it "must be nice." Those people were not the ones I needed.

I learned to strategically only tell people that I knew would offer high-fives. Putting my dream out into the world before it was ready felt like putting my face out there on Tinder for someone to swipe left.

I don't need that kind of negativity in my life.

I've learned to keep big hairy goals to myself for as long as I need. I tell people who I know have my back and keep it safe — a small group of business owners and friends who get me. Then, I go out, do the work, and make it happen.

Of all the lessons I learned before quitting my corporate job, this one was probably the hardest and the most important.

They say you take on the qualities of the five people you spend the most time with. Jim Rohn famously talked about how the money you make is an average of the incomes of the five people you spend most of your time with. When I heard this, I woke the fuck up and started to get serious.

At the time, I was spending my time with some broke-ass people. People who were always complaining about not having money to do anything.

This might sound shallow, but it's not so much about the money as it is about what the money represents — ambition, goals, and life experiences.

How in the world do you take your life and business to a higher level when you surround yourself with complainers, blamers, and people who are perfectly content with mediocrity?

Trick question. The answer is — you don't.

This was a hard change to step into.

The first part of the lesson involved the people I was spending time with. After a particular evening where another mom did nothing but complain and gossip about other moms, I realized I had to use my time and energy more effectively.

This was not an easy decision, but I had to cut some people away. I slowly started removing myself from those conversations and stopped engaging.

It even came down to Jacob's sports. When he was nine, he said to us one night about his hockey team, "Mom, my team isn't very good." He was ready for an up-level too. If my kid turned out to be the average of the five people he spent the most time with, then he was not going to gain many skills in the sport he loves.

He wanted a new team. I wanted familiar faces and predictability. I like comfort. I don't like quitting people or teams. I don't like confrontation.

Jacob wanted to try out for a better team in another hockey

club, and we let him. And when I say try out, he tried his ass off. He played three consecutive nights of tryouts like his life depended on it. Which I can't imagine is actually a thing when you're nine. But he did. And he made it.

I was so proud of him. He had to do a little leveling up of his own. I was beyond uncomfortable just telling people about it. *What would the team we were leaving think? Would they hate us for leaving?* Well, the answer was mostly yes — a few people sent us nasty emails about how we were terrible parents and were damaging him. The politics in kids' sports is no joke. I'll save those stories for another book (that one's in process).

Jacob was happier for the change. It was awkward at first: meeting a new team, new coaches, new families. It was uncomfortable, painful, and stressful and caused me to lose sleep a few nights, but it was worth it. He leveled-up, ended up on a better team, made friends (which he would have done anyway), and so did we.

When you have a small selection of people to hang out with, you need to choose the best you possibly can. This doesn't mean you won't lift people up who don't have the privilege you have — with money, time, or other resources.

Life felt more fun when I stopped hanging around the negative nellies and decided to make time to schedule nights out with the friends who seemed more positive, who had goals, and who were committed to doing interesting things. I have nothing against a little complaining. What I have a problem with is when the only conversation you can have with some people is about other people.

Small talk is painful enough for me as an introvert. Make me talk for an hour about drama, fights, and judgments, and I'm going to want to stab my eyeballs out.

Instead, I started surrounding myself with people who were having conversations about big ideas, experiences, change, and making a difference — whether in their world, or their family.

When things don't feel right, I know to trust my gut — I'm probably not in the right place.

If I don't feel like I belong, and I don't even *want* to try, it's not a place for me. When I can't even muster up the slightest bit of give a fuck, it's not my circus. When conversation physically hurts and feels so dull that I have to fight to stay awake — it's not my place.

Not my motherloving circus. Time to find a new circus.

Chances are, if you're anything like me, you've probably been hanging around the right people all along, and just didn't notice. I promise once you think about yourself surrounded by the five people you spend the most time with or your most energy on, you'll look at investing your time in a new light. If you don't already have these people in your immediate circles, they're probably not far away.

There are so many ways to find your people. Mentally list the people who are in your life, both online and off. Feel free to separate the two if it feels easier. If you're scrolling through your social media feed and someone's posts produce tension in your body or make you feel jealousy, insecurity, angst, anger, or other negative feelings, unfollow them until you can figure out what it is that bothers you.

Same with the people you see in the flesh. Are there people you see every day that make you feel tired, drained, and empty? They might not be your people.

I know I'm in good company if, after hours of talking, I feel energized.

It's not easy in a world of small talk and niceties to choose only to have conversations that feel good in your bones.

Because if not, you're going to end up in someone else's shit show of a circus.

When you take a stand for what you believe in, it will feel scary. You might feel completely alone. This is okay and entirely normal.

When you strive for more, that's where you'll find the magic. Without the striving, you're stuck in the same old circus with the same old monkeys.

Our thoughts are a shitty boss

Here's where my thoughts go when I let them run around pantless in my mind:

You suck.

You're going to fail at this, why even bother?

No one cares about you or your book — this is so dumb.

Only famous people write memoirs, this is so indulgent.

You're faking it, and everyone is going to know.

You should just quit now.

So and so is way better at this than you, let them do it.

They're going to hate it.

If the voice in your head doesn't say these things to you, please tell me your secrets.

The first layoff shook my confidence. *What if it happened again?* Well it did, twice. I wondered if I could use the layoffs to become more confident in starting my business. My business could still fail, but there was a huge difference when it was just me in charge. I was in control. In a corporate setting, I had some power, sure, but the direction of the business, the strategic decisions, they were all out of my hands. In my business, I can pay attention to what's happening and pivot quickly if I need to turn it around or go left or go right.

It doesn't matter how long you've been doing what you're doing. Even if you're a master or goddess who's so good at your craft that people pay you all the dollars and you have a waiting list as long as a vineyard — this voice is still there. It gets smaller and quieter over time as you learn to tell it to take a walk. I'm not sure we can ever completely squash the self-doubt monster, but we can find ways to thank it and carry on.

There are some things we can do to turn the volume down on that voice in our heads so that a Whisper 2000 can barely detect it.

One of my favorites is the cancel process. While I'm usually thoughtful with my words, sometimes my mouth moves faster than my brain, and I say something stupid or out of line. *Wait! I take that back!* Well, I do the same with my thinking. When a thought creeps up that dulls my shine, I say something in my head like *cancel, cancel, cancel*, or *delete, delete, delete*, or *reject and delete*.

Then, I get to tell a better story.

You are in charge of your thoughts. You can change them whenever you like. Hear a load of crap in your ear? Stop that thought and tell yourself another one. You don't have to be all fairy dust about it and tell yourself that you're a sparkly rainbow of luminous delight. Use words you'd use with friends after two glasses of wine, like "Hey, this is completely normal, do better next time."

I also have a thank bank that I deposit praise, kind emails, and kudos into regularly. I keep mine in a Google Doc and in a special email folder that I literally named "Thank Bank." Every time I get a gushing email, or a small note of thanks or praise, I take a copy and store it in my thank bank. On days when my thoughts are running wild, I make a mistake, or actually do suck at something, I read through my thank bank and feel so much better.

Beyond showering myself in gratitude, sharing gratitude outward gives me an instant boost. Sometimes I write a thank-you note on a card and drop it in the mail, send a nice email, or write a review of a favorite restaurant.

In addition, consider getting a coach, a therapist, and some friends who will check your limiting thoughts at the door. Even better, get all three — remember, you become the essence of the five people you spend the most time with.

For most of my life I tried to go it alone. The lone warrior, I always had an idea that asking for help made me weak. I'm still unraveling those behaviors. The more you ask for help, the more you realize that people *want* to help. Especially when those people are good at it.

Here's what my support network looks like these days — Ryan holding up the other end of our household in his career, striving for more and better, and pushing me to be better. My kids to show me where I need to work on myself, and for them to do chores around the house (for this reason, a housekeeper is not yet part of my support system). A paid mastermind because I don't want to be the smartest person in a room. Business besties — friends I can text in the middle of the day when I'm stuck or need to bounce my latest idea off someone. A coach — who's supported me in wiping out negative emotions (yeah, I didn't think it was possible either) and showing me how to train my brain to expect good things. My work with my coach has been a game changer. My family, who I can always count on. Even though we're five hundred miles away, they're my number one fans.

An objective opinion will be able to spot a negative thought spiral a mile away and can help you reframe it. And it takes practice. I've spent more than a decade consciously looking at my thoughts, and there's still some gunk that comes up in there from time to time. It's going to happen — I can use the opportunity to strengthen my mind, and over time, it becomes a habit.

You've got a masterpiece to create

When I was first thinking about starting a business — remember, eight whole years before I had enough momentum to take it full time, I spent months trying to figure it out by staring at my computer, filling out worksheets, and downloading every free PDF on the internet — I was doing a lot of things that made me *feel* like I was building something but didn't actually take me any further down the road. I was desperate to finally figure out what it was that I wanted to do with my life. It was as if someone else or something outside of me had all the answers.

Night after night, I'd eat an inappropriate amount of chocolate and drink just a little more wine than I'd planned. I'd have an idea — I'm going to only write about hummus! I wish I was joking. I thought I was going to build a business around dip. Now, I believe you can create a business around just about anything. Building a thriving income around dip might have been a stretch, though.

I'd get super-stoked about an idea. Then I would tell literally one person, they'd scoff, I'd doubt myself, and I'd squash my concept. Back to the couch. One person thinks it sucks. Someone laughed; someone doesn't get it. Someone tells me I'll never make any money and my idea is a waste of time.

I'd do this over and over and over again. It only started working when I stopped seeking validation. Not only was I asking the wrong people — Ryan, who is not my target audience — I also wasn't thinking about what I really wanted to do. I was trying to find something, anything, to help me start my career over.

If I could go back to that girl on the couch eating too much chocolate, I'd tell her to get her ass off the motherloving couch and try something. Try anything — it's the only way to figure out what will feel good.

When I finally started, it was a food blog; then it was a lifestyle blog, then a blog and a mini-book for working moms, meal plans, then cooking classes, then freelance copywriting, then coaching.

Before I could create any kind of momentum, I overanalyzed every single move. It's like I was taking a magnifying glass to my life. I'd judge the tiniest thing, or worse, let someone else do the judging, and if what they had to say wasn't what I was hoping to hear, I'd move on. I wouldn't be crushed about it — I just couldn't move forward without a cheering section.

When I started my first website, I'd write a page then run it by a handful of people. Sometimes they were friends, colleagues I trusted, or even randos on the internet. They'd judge every word and paragraph, and then pick apart the graphics and website layout — which is so beyond my comfort zone and my skills.

If I wasn't completely clear on my next step or exactly what I was doing, I'd end up stuck. Stuck and paralyzed — so I'd do nothing. The notebooks full of ideas would sit untouched, sometimes for years.

My ideas about this book were only mine for years. I realized I was sharing too soon, and my ideas needed time to marinate first. I was so worried about every little move that I didn't even know what made me smile anymore. How do I uncouple the stress of every little thing and notice what feels right? I had to step back and see the entire painting to identify my favorite parts.

I used to love drawing as a kid. I'd spend hours as a kid with my bedroom door closed, working on a single sketch for days. Then, someone said something about one of my drawings. "That doesn't really look right." And I put the pencil down. I didn't pick it back up for more than ten years. *What's the point? I'm not the best.*

It's as if someone was standing over my shoulder as I slowly drew the first line on the page.

Wait — stop! You're not using enough pressure. It needs to be a #6 pencil. That line isn't long enough. What are you drawing anyway? You should angle your pencil a little closer to the paper. How are you going to market that? Everything you make needs to make money. You don't have time for hobbies, you need to launch, grow, scale, and blow up your business!

What in the actual fuck? I don't even know what I'm going to draw yet, but you're over my shoulder criticizing every pencil stroke? Ah, fuck it. I suck, I should just put it down.

Imagine you're standing over my shoulder as I dip my brush in the acrylic, then tentatively, after a sip of red wine, I add some color to my blank canvas.

"STOP!" you yell.
"That color is repulsive!"
"You didn't make a long enough brush stroke."
"You didn't have enough paint on your brush!"
"What are you even doing?"
"It's ugly."
"I hate it."
"You suck."

Could you imagine doing that to a painter?
Same thing goes for a writer, designer, and hair stylist.
For the love of all things full of wine, I hope not.

Then, why on earth would you do this to yourself? Or for your work?

You don't criticize a painter for every brushstroke — you admire the painting when it's finished.

Where do you draw the line between constructive coaching and judging every little thing? How can you take a step back from your game, your craft, your life, and give yourself a pat on the back and move forward?

And trust that the entire painting isn't complete at the end of a game; it's complete after the end of a season, after five years, or ten, or never.

Now, imagine all the stuff you say in your head about your work. The thing you're afraid to put out there. Listen closely, and you'll notice you might be judging every little thing.

All the judgment might be leaving no room to possibly create anything. You might not be finishing anything because you can't get started. It all feels impossible.

Take a step back — or thirty. In life and business, avoid criticizing yourself (or anyone else, for that matter) based on every blog post, botched introduction, awkward interaction, or the time you opened your mouth too soon.

Judging a book by its cover is one thing. Would you judge a book by a single page, a sentence, or even a word? Judge every book by the opening line, and you might never read another book again.

Have patience to consider your long game. Your entire life season. You wouldn't toss an entire baseball season because one swing was too high, and you wouldn't quit your business because of one bad hiring decision. Get on with your life and keep moving forward.

Your work is a painting.

Your life is a painting.

Hopefully, you'll look at it more like a masterpiece and less like a hot mess.

Every move you make is a brushstroke. It's all part of your body of work, your life's work.

When you do this, you'll be less critical of yourself. That little voice in your head telling you that you suck? You'll be able to tell it to shut up and eventually, redirect it and give it some newer, more positive, and supporting language.

You've got painting to do.

Motivation isn't the problem

During a trip to Boston for one summer with the family, we noticed a crowd outside the famous downtown Granary Burying Ground. The kids were fascinated with the signs for cemeteries and ghost tours. They wanted to know if they were haunted. They also amused us with questions like, "Is everyone in there dead?"

Tentatively I answered, "I think so."

Walking past the graveyard, I felt a pang of curiosity as I recalled a quote from *Die Empty*, by Todd Henry: "The most valuable land in the world is the graveyard. In the graveyard are buried all of the unwritten novels, never-launched businesses, unreconciled relationships, and all of the other things that people thought, 'I'll get around to that tomorrow.' One day, however, their tomorrows ran out." Dying empty doesn't mean literally emptying yourself every single day. It's about getting your best work out of you, living in a way you feel good about, and slipping under the covers with a happy, shit-eating grin every day.

Did these people die empty? This is also where Paul Revere and Samuel Adams are buried. *Did they die empty? Did they have ideas and dreams inside of them that never saw the light of day before they were laid to rest?*

Then, my curiosity turned to sadness as I thought about the possible magnitude of the unfulfilled potential in the graveyard. That curiosity rang through my mind for the rest of the day. How many people did I pass on the street (especially in Boston's financial district, with all the scrunched up, serious faces) who aren't doing what they want to be doing? How many people have a half-written book that they haven't touched in a year, or ten? How many people have something important to say to someone but are too scared? How many people are afraid to be vulnerable? Are they living in fear of being judged?

When I used to climb into bed feeling dissatisfied at the end of every day, I'd wake up with an even greater sense of dread with the buzz of the morning alarm.

Ugh. What's the point? As I switched off the alarm and thought about all the things I needed to do that day, my mind raced — racing nowhere and spinning my wheels on a train that was speeding toward the light at the end of the tunnel.

When my train gets to the end of the tunnel of light, I wondered if I would feel good about my life or feel full of regrets.

It was after I read *Die Empty* that I wrote my first mini-book. I wrote it like a speed demon in just two months. I wrote it like I desperately had a message to get out. I'm glad I did it, and I'm very proud that I made it happen (even if many of my opinions from that time have changed). If I hadn't read *Die Empty*, I might still be boring my friends by saying, "I'd love to write a book someday." (And you might not be holding this one in your hands now).

I don't want to die with all my best ideas in my head. I don't want to die with half a dozen unfinished book projects. I want to die knowing I did my damn best to empty out. Get it out into the world even if it sucks — even if everyone hates it. Even if all my ideas and opinions change.

When staring down a big project, our thoughts can run wild:

I need more motivation.
I'm not motivated.
If I could just find the motivation.
I need to find the willpower.
Where the heck do you get motivation and willpower?

Those were the problems I thought I had when I was first struggling to start my own business. But it turned out I had a much bigger problem — I was doing all the wrong things.

In my life and in my work.

By sitting around thinking about a hummus business instead of taking a single step toward creating a business — any business — I was showing myself that I wasn't serious. If it really mattered, I would have started that business, done the thing, showed up, and stood out. Eventually, I did, and while I hung out in no-man's-land for many years, my only regret was that I didn't take imperfect action sooner.

Now, I know I'm on the right track because I've made a bigger promise to myself to die a little emptier, and I go to bed most nights with a smile. Hands on my heart, I smile and think, "Holy shit, this is my life. Thank you."

In the three-ish years it took to write and finish this book, I can tell you that when I wasn't working on it, I was thinking about it and feeling deep regret for ignoring it. It was only during the months of focused writing, rewriting, and editing that I felt immensely satisfied. Even when the words felt funky and the sentences tedious, I felt aligned and completely congruent in my work and life values.

Dig deeper into why you haven't done the things that keep you up at night. You're getting these nudges for a reason.

What do you need to do right now, today, or this week, so you can die just a little emptier?

Do that.

What do you want to be known for?

If I'm going to be known for one thing, what will I do every day? How will I structure my day? Now, that one thing has certainly changed over the years, and it will likely change again.

I want to be known for making writing easier for people. Unfussy writing, at the heart, is getting writing done and making it feel easy and approachable.

If I want to be known for helping people write what's on their hearts, then how I invest my time matters — namely, doing my own writing.

Two years into my freelance copywriting career, I realized that I wasn't becoming known for being a writer. I was known for being a *copywriter* — someone who writes words for other people.

I love my clients, and my favorite part of our work together is collaborating, strategizing, and becoming an unofficial partner in their businesses. While copywriting was what initially helped me replace my corporate income, something was off.

I wasn't writing for myself anymore. Sure, I was publishing blog articles each week, sharing content in weekly emails and social media, while this book sat collecting electronic dust. Not to mention the two other books I had already started.

Creating content on-demand for others is fun and challenging and stretches my brain in the best way. And yet, I wasn't prioritizing my passion projects. I'd push my book writing to the bottom of the list if it even made it on the list at all. Night after night, I'd either forget about my project or sit down on the couch exhausted and with no creativity left to write a damn word of my own.

I wondered how I could do both business and my creative work because I realized that when I take the time to fill my creative tank and work on a passion project, I show up as a better human for my clients. Not to mention wife and mom too.

I connected the dots — by writing my books, I can get my clients better results. When I recommitted to finishing this book, I set myself up for success. I scheduled an hour a day, three times a week to work on my book. I planned thirty days on the calendar and made adjustments for the time of day — for a few months. Then, throughout the year, I wrote it as the number one item on my daily paper planner: "Book." I'd revise at least a chapter or two each day. And then, for even more accountability, I put an out-of-office note on my social media accounts and went dark for a month.

Then, inside my online writing community, I created a daily word count tracker. We tracked our word count daily in a spreadsheet. As the host and writing coach inside this community, this was an opportunity for me to be visible and share my progress. I shared progress updates with community members and offered up insights into what was working for my daily habit.

Lastly, I recorded a series of videos on my phone when my writing was finished. I recorded a new video each day, missing only one, with a behind-the-scenes peek into how I was making this work a part of my day and the emotions and thoughts that came up along the way. Sometimes I'd remember the video as I lay in bed and would record it right there with my head on the pillow.

All of these checkpoints added a few minutes of tasks to my day, but without them, I wonder how successful I'd be.

Know what you want to be known for and behave accordingly. If I want to be known as a leader who helps people make the time for writing and helps make that writing easier — *I need to write.*

The unfussiest writer in the world would make the time to refill the creative well. They'd eat good food and enjoy their wine every single evening. They'd sit at the page for at least fifteen minutes, no matter what.

VI. TRUSTING MY INTUITION

"Whatever emotional experience has made you who you are today is where you will find the seeds of your life purpose."

Lauren Sapala, *The INFJ Writer: Cracking the Creative Genius of the World's Rarest Type*

When I give you advice, dear reader, it's really only me talking to myself in the past. Based on my experiences and lessons, this section contains advice for becoming more you. I am changing every second of every day. And so are you. By the time you read this, I've changed some more. This is the beauty of the human experience.

They're here to suck your blood

Energy vampires suck the energy, and sometimes your will to live, right out of your soul. You'll know you've met an energy vampire if after spending an evening, or even fifteen minutes, with them you feel exhausted. After a brief conversation, you're suddenly tired; you hate your life, your hair, your job, and even your knees.

Weird, how did that even happen? You need a protective shield from those energy sucks until you can get them out of your life. They're not necessarily bad people — maybe just bad for you.

In the online world, that's why every social media app has an unfollow option. The unfriend option, of course, is the more blatant message that someone has been sucking up all your energy, and you're not going to take it anymore. Use the block option for people who are downright toxic or harmful.

In the online world, we can mute the whiners, complainers, attention seekers, and commiserators. In real life (IRL), it's trickier. You see that shit-disturber on the other side of the room at a party, and you can stay in your corner, talking to people who energize you.

Speaking of sitting in my corner, it wasn't until I was well into my thirties that I finally began to embrace my introversion. As a kid, the grown-ups would often ask me, "Why are you so quiet?"

The extroverted world is finally starting to understand us introverts a little better — well, the ones who get quiet enough to notice anyway. Shy, quiet, reserved, level-headed — whatever label you want to apply, I'm fine with it.

Introversion isn't about being quiet or disliking people. Sometimes I'm loud, and like most people, I need to balance it with more subdued, deep conversations and more people I enjoy than dislike. Being an introvert isn't about liking people or not, it's about how sensitive you are to external stimuli. Lots of external stimuli can tend to drain an introvert's energy, so they then recharge by reducing the number of people, level of noise, or amount of movement around them.

I can stand on a stage, I can be (awkward) on camera, I can go to events in large conference halls, and I can enjoy the spotlight. I'll be the one who will look for one really great connection instead of coming home with a blazer-pocket full of business cards, and then I'll retreat to the couch under the heaviest blanket I can find with the fullest glass of wine and watch some light-hearted bullshit on Netflix.

And, as an intuitive introvert, known as an INFJ in Myers-Briggs framework, the better I manage the energy I let in, the better I can manage the energy I put out into the world.

So, while I perhaps unfairly call the people who steal my energy 'energy vampires,' it's not their fault, it's mine — for leaving my energy door flapping in the wind.

The first step is recognizing who drains you and who energizes you. When I was living in Illinois, I had a group of friends I'd meet for wine, dinners out, or painting. These were the kinds of friends who I'd linger with at a restaurant, long after we've finished the last bite of flourless chocolate cake.

It takes a while to make new friends as an adult, especially when you've moved as many times as I have. Without kids, I'm really not sure how I'd make new friends. Some of my greatest friendships came from hockey experiences. Hockey moms naturally spend a lot of time together — practice three times a week, two games on the weekend, and entire weekends together for out-of-town tournaments. It's that kind of intense togetherness that's helped me forge deeper friendships in adulthood.

One hockey tournament that stands out in my mind was in the Wisconsin Dells. It's a tourist trap centered around half a dozen or so indoor water parks. Imagine stripping down to your swimsuit and drinking strawberry daiquiris in a chlorinated, bleached, ninety-degree, hundred percent humidity indoor pool that's overrun with kids in swim diapers. Oh, and you're going to spend three days there and attend at least four hockey games.

I didn't even pack the kids' swimsuits or tell them what the Dells was all about. And when some of the kids were screaming in pain at 10:00 p.m. from the chemical burns, I knew I'd made the right choice.

This was also the year that our head coach would drink too much with some other parents. We're talking about dads puking in the parking lot before games and screaming matches between parents and coaches.

Being around this kind of energy depleted me. It was at this tournament that a few moms who I had been close to would catch each other in the hotel hallways and say, "I'm not into this water park business, there's a good restaurant across the street — what do you say we skip out on the spring break vibe and enjoy a quiet dinner?"

One mom got on the phone to make reservations for a handful of families right away.

After enjoying a lively dinner — though much more subdued than the pool — we returned to the hotel to find many of the other parents drinking in the hallway (totally not judging because I do that too). Another parent asked us to join them.

But on this particular evening, after catching wind of all the drama the previous evening, I had another idea.

"How about we hang out in our room instead?"

That evening, while the kids played quietly in the next room, us moms got to talking about our goals and dreams. We talked about what we'd do for work if money was no object.

One mom, an attorney, would start a healing center. Another, in banking, would work with animals.

At that time, I had recently given notice at my corporate job and was about to take my part-time side-hustle and turn it into my full-time business.

I thought about my reply. "Hmm, I'm already doing it."

With a group full of drunk parents, I don't think I would have landed on this vulnerable conversation. Because I trusted what I needed most — a soul-nurturing, quiet conversation with people who listen, and people I want to listen to.

Up until the time we moved to New Jersey, these were the friendships I'd treasure. And really, they were the first honest and totally genuine friendships I'd really made since getting married and leaving my hometown.

We'd get together as often as our full schedules allowed. By the time we moved, our sons all played on different teams. And instead of talking about other people, we talked about what excited us: books, work, and creativity.

Anytime we met up for a paint night at my house or out for dinner, they'd be the events that I'd look forward to all week. At the end of most evenings at home, I find myself in bed by 9:00 p.m. When I was together with these moms, I'd come home at 11:00 and feel energized and inspired to stay up even later.

On the flip side, after thirty minutes of a corporate work party where I was encouraged to "go make as many connections as you can" (actual instructions from my boss), you might wonder where I went. I left, quickly, without saying goodbye, and I was probably halfway home before anyone noticed.

Figure out who your energy amplifiers are, the people you

like, and begin to understand the difference. You don't need to be a jerk about it. You can simply avoid hanging out with them or bring some more positive people along when you're going to be in their company. I often imagine myself in an invisible protective bubble if I know I'll be around a lot of people or spending time in a city. The bubble protects my good, clean energy that I've worked so hard to create and keeps bad vibes out.

Remember, you become like the five people you spend the most time with. When you get better, the people around you get better, and when you lift other people up, you'll feel good about yourself and your life too. It's a winning game for everyone. Even those vamps could want some of whatever you're having, and then you helped create a positive change for them too.

You might have to have some hard conversations as you swap the energy vampires in your life for more positive people.

When you turn people down a few times (my go-to, passive approach), they'll usually get the picture, but if they're not getting it — you might need to speak up and let them know that you think you've grown apart.

And whatever you do, please don't actually call them an energy vampire — this won't make anyone feel good.

And what if *you* are the energy vampire? If perception is projection, there may be some information in there for you too. If people grate on your nerves, ask yourself, "How is this me?" When my coach asks me this, I have a love-hate response. *Uh, but I don't want it to be me.*

Well, that certainly sucks. Just kidding, there's still hope. You might be sucking the will to live from others if you notice people who used to talk a lot suddenly don't have that much to share with you anymore. Maybe they cancel plans or stop calling.

Ask yourself how much you're complaining. Are you a constant whiner? Do you have anything good to say about anyone or anything? How well do you listen? Do you constantly have some kind of drama going on in your life, and you can't seem to understand why?

Then you might be an energy vampire.

It's not just people — specific tasks and places can suck your energy too. When we have less energy, we can't do the things we want to do.

In many companies, employees bounce from meeting to meeting without pausing to take a breath. If you're the kind of person who thrives on being around people and having conversations all day, then this might sound like a dream. If not, this is probably going to leave you feeling wiped out. When I was in my nine-to-five, I'd plan breaks in my day to recharge if I could — slipping in my earbuds was my go-to ritual. Sometimes I would simply leave them in with nothing playing. And on days I couldn't, I'd recharge during my commute with an inspiring audiobook.

Misaligned work will feel like an energy vampire. For me, that's making me look at spreadsheets all day or fighting a backend problem with my website. At times when this tedious work is unavoidable, I tackle these things at the very end of my workday, or on a dedicated day of the week like Friday.

It's also important to notice the times when you've felt excited to dive into your work. Was there a particular morning in the past few weeks you couldn't wait to get to work because you were stoked to get started on something?

Maybe you get energy from solving a problem, or it might be working with certain people that gives you that jolt of energy you're after. Maybe you gel really well with a particular colleague and can't wait to collaborate on another project. This could be your sweet spot for great work with great people. The more you can fill your life with the kinds of people and projects that have you popping out of bed in the morning, the better your quality of work will be.

When you can get excited about your work and even certain tasks — this is where the magic is. Follow that magic and good feelings down a rabbit hole and see where it takes you. Following these nudges are what led me to finally stepping away from corporate work and starting my business. And I continue to follow them, refining and tweaking all the areas of my business so work feels more fun and meaningful than ever.

Drink the good wine

When Jacob was seven, he played one season of baseball (thankfully, it was only a single season — that's one boring sport). After an evening game, we visited one of the parents' homes along with twenty or so other parents and their rowdy kids. I settled in at the basement bar, one of the first to arrive, and the hostess asked me what I'd like to drink.

"Red wine, please." My standard unfussy answer. Occasionally I'll ask for white wine if it's a hot summer afternoon.

This was when things got awkward.

I watched our hosts scrambling behind the bar, looking for wine. There were at least two dozen bottles right in plain sight. Confused, I figured the bottles I was looking at were all white wine.

I'm flexible. "If you can't find red, white is fine too," I told them.

The host responded, "Oh, it's not that. We have lots of red, but only expensive bottles and no 'every day' wine. You understand, right?" They searched my face for some confirmation.

Well, they wouldn't find it. What the fuck? "Yeah, okay. No worries."

I sat at the bar, making casual conversation with other

parents who I'd only chatted with a few times, while the hosts continued the search party, spanning two floors of their four-thousand-square-foot home, for "inexpensive" wine. I was about to call the whole search off and drink water instead. This went on for an awkwardly long time.

Eventually, the host presented a bottle of Chianti.

Yes! "Chianti is perfect!"

Turns out I wasn't meant to drink from that bottle. The host told me when I was halfway through my glass that the wine he gave me was "from an expensive bottle of wine because it was on the shelf where we normally keep the cheap ones."

I'm thinking, okay, should I say, "thank you?" Do they want me to pay them for their "expensive" wine?

"It's good wine, thank you." Really though, it wasn't worth the fuss, and I am not a fussy grape-lover. As I finished the last sip, and the host just stared at my empty glass, I assumed a refill was out of the question. I already drank more of the good wine than I was supposed to.

I said a few quick goodbyes, thanked the hosts, and got the hell out of there. I felt gross.

From my perspective, there I was in a lovely home with all the high ceilings, granite, and stainless steel one could dream of, a fully stocked bar, and some luxury cars parked in the oversized garage. To the naked eye, these people appeared to have everything. But not enough to share with me. Or they were saving the good wine for better company.

In case you think I'm a wine snob, I'm not. If it comes in a bottle or even a box, I'm happy. I'll drink from your $6 bottle and your $150 bottle with the same delight.

Treat everyone with the same respect, whether it's your new friend, your favorite uncle, your $100 a month client or a client that just dropped $20,000 on a coaching package.

Give *everyone* the good wine.

Here's the most important part: Don't, for the love of dark salty caramel chocolate, tell them you're giving them the good wine. Just pour the motherloving wine (and maybe a second glass).

There are no "special occasions." They're all special occasions. Treat every single guest and every single client with the same level of attention. Don't hold out for a "special" client or an epic event. It may never come.

Think about all the things you're saving for a special day. Over the years of moving, downsizing, paring down, and being intentional with everything in my house, there's no such thing as saving the good soap, keeping dishes I only use "sometimes," and especially wine that I only drink on special occasions.

If it's in the house, it's fair game.

Have you ever met someone who celebrates seemingly small things, like making a new sports team, working out for five consecutive days, or landing a big project at work? They're ordering the champagne on a random Tuesday night just 'cause. They're here to enjoy the moment and enjoy their life.

That would be me.

When I order champagne at a restaurant, often the server asks, "What's the occasion?"

My answer varies: "Life," or "It's Wednesday," or "I like to celebrate every day."

People are going to notice. It's not every Monday at noon that your server gets to grab the prosecco out of the cellar.

Give it a try. I promise if you bust out the "good dishes" on a Monday night (assuming you didn't KonMari them already), put on a sexy outfit, cook the filet mignon, put out the fancy ketchup, and pop the cork on the expensive champagne you've been saving for a "special day," you'll feel like a badass. Feeling like a badass will bring you more badass experiences.

Live your life every day like it's a bit of a celebration. Because you know what? It is. If you can't celebrate the small moments, the big ones might never feel big enough. When is a moment significant enough to celebrate? Does it need to have a specific dollar amount or achievement level attached to it? Consider celebrating effort, progress, and the journey rather than the destination.

Becoming the person who's known for celebrating every little accomplishment and event is far from being a bad thing. You just might attract more badass friends.

Think of all the seemingly small things in your life that could stand to have a little upgrade. Going from an unscented white bar of soap to the local handmade coconut oil soap with tiny flakes of ground up coffee beans could take your morning shower from mundane to er-ma-gerd! Who doesn't need exfoliating coffee beans in their life? I don't know about you, but the first ten minutes of my day is pretty important. I'm going to lather up my hot naked bod with something that feels good.

When it comes time for your morning coffee — are you just drinking your coffee because it has some kind of a job to do? Do you even enjoy the stuff you're putting in your mouth? If you're not, it might be time for a little upgrade. Just switching from instant to an organic local roaster might feel fancy, and it might be the smallest shift you need to feel like you're living a rich life.

Maybe good coffee doesn't excite you, but the vessel itself does. Every coffee cup in my cabinet feels good to use. The second any of my dishes get a chip in them, I toss them. It's my first sip of the day that's going to power me up to take on the world, and it's going to feel good. There are lots of mismatched dishes in my cabinets, and not a single full set. If a dinner guest judges me on it, they get the boxed wine (totally kidding).

I buy plenty of bottles of ten-dollar wine. But I'll spend more on occasion, and I drink it. I splurge on good chocolate and eat the chocolate. The funny thing is that the good stuff tastes better and satisfies the craving quicker, so I consume less.

It's the shrimp ring you were saving for company or even eating dinner in the room that you usually only reserve for special guests. It's sitting there and enjoying your meal on a Tuesday night with the soft napkins instead of a scratchy paper towel, using the crystal and slathering on the motherloving Grey Poupon because you want to — and that reason is good enough.

When you spend the money, buy the thing, do the work, say yes, pop the cork, and celebrate all wins (big and small), you're telling the universe what's up and showing that bitch that you have room for more good experiences in your life. The abundance that flows out, flows right back in.

How do you think your company will feel when they come to your home for the first time and notice you've used your good dishes and are drinking the good wine? You might be worried that you're setting the bar too high, and they'll expect this level of delicious food and wine every time they come over for salmon steaks, and maybe that's okay. Treat all guests like royalty. It's not about them returning the favor or showing off or keeping up with the Joneses.

It's about showing up every day with what you've got. The best for yourself and everyone — regardless of who they are or how much money they make.

Treating yourself in small ways every single day is where the magic is. It will do something major for your life too — it will shift your entire perspective to one that piques the curiosity of everyone around you. You're special because you believe enough in yourself to treat yourself to the best that you can enjoy — whatever that is.

Watch the damn sunset

While on a family vacation in Treasure Island, Florida, Ryan and I dropped the kids off at my mother-in-law's and hit up a highly rated steakhouse for date night.

Halfway through the jumbo sea scallops appetizer, I reminded Ryan that we hadn't seen a Treasure Island sunset together in more than thirteen years — since we visited while engaged all those years ago.

Before we had kids, we'd returned to Florida to the scene of the crime — the VIP Mexican restaurant and bar. This was still the pre-smartphone era. Instead of snapping pictures of our adventures and instantly posting them for the world to see, we simply were there together. We'd take in the sights, and grab pictures on the beach with a camera — the kind that doesn't vibrate.

That evening at the steakhouse (kid-free but not smartphone-free), I begged him to sit on the beach and enjoy the sunset with me. And he didn't want to go. He whined — a lot. "I'm tired," and "I don't want to get all sandy."

I dismissed his whining with a wave of my hand and said, "Shut up, you're watching the sunset with me. Let's go."

And off we went. He sat there, feeling resentful for a minute, only there to please me, but I didn't care. I ignored him — I was there for my sunset dammit.

As far as sunsets go, it was perfect. A flurry of red, orange, pink, and yellow crisscrossed the sky. It was relaxing, calm, and serene, complete with the warm salty breeze you'd expect to mess up your hair as it blew off the gulf — because sexy beach hair. And we were on a legit date! Granted, Ryan had just consumed all fifty-something ounces of the tomahawk steak at the steakhouse (barf) and was probably too busy digesting that dead animal to appreciate much else.

It was a sunset that made you feel all the feels that sunsets are supposed to stir up.

Sitting back on a public bench, watching the free color show, we noticed dozens of people were power walking from the boardwalk to jump on the sand to catch the same sunset. They all looked like they were in a hurry, and I didn't get it. Sun's still there, folks.

They all had their smartphones in hand, ready to take a selfie as if their lives depended on it.

I wondered what the selfie-takers were saying.

"I was here, look at me, I'm the kind of person that watches sunsets, and brings my phone because — the internet. And look how cool I am at this sunset. I love nature."

Couples were standing next to one another, both of them with their phones in hand snapping identical sunset pics. Families were sitting together with one parent ignoring their kids and taking pictures of the sky.

I've been guilty of this, which is why it had such an impact on me when I could sit back and observe. It looks like my mind being in another place when Talia is in gymnastics class or Jacob is at hockey.

It looks like never actually wanting to be where I am in the moment.

If you've ever snapped a picture of a sunset and captioned it with something like "the picture doesn't do it justice," you'd be right. Your phone will never capture the essence of a sunset. Never.

It may create a reminder for you of the sunset you watched that one time in Treasure Island. But you will miss the feeling. THE feeling that happens in that precise moment where you stand, hands-free mode, watching, listening, feeling, and sensing.

Next time, I dare you. Watch the damn sunset. And if you must take a picture — take a quick few, then tuck your phone away so you can be there. You can post it later.

There's no prize for being the most social

A few years ago, I traveled to Toronto from Chicago to celebrate Jen's thirtieth birthday. In case you're wondering, I'm the older and much wiser sibling.

Ryan missed out on all the fun since he had a big-ass motorcycle rally to attend. Hundreds of bearded, leather-clad men drinking beer and eating fried food off floppy paper plates — no thank you. This meant I was flying solo with the kids. For a moment, I considered Benadryl to knock them out on the flight, but that stuff can sometimes produce the opposite effect of what you're hoping for.

Crazy, wired kids packed into an aluminum tube at thirty thousand feet? Nope! I opted for being armed with new toys, enough snacks to feed all the other passengers *and* the crew, and, most importantly, a calm mind. When we sat down, a flight attendant approached me, grabbed my arm with the grip of death, crouched down, and said, "Listen, I'm a parent, and I know this is going to be terrible."

I raised an eyebrow. What I wanted to say was, *Dude! Shut up! No, it's not!* What I did manage to say through a forced smile was, "Thank you." The kids were happy, and it was only my thoughts about the event that would make it terrible. I'd show him.

The sixty-minute flight was great, and the kids were content. We landed, I shot a message to my dad (my ride), and put my phone in my pocket so I'd have easy access later. We deplaned and got in line for inspection by Canadian immigration. Patting my pockets, I noticed my phone was missing. We were in a room with doors that locked both in front of and behind me. There was literally no turning back — we were trapped.

I approached an airline attendee before speaking to the immigration officer, and after he made a few phone calls to the gate, he said he regretted informing me that the plane I was on had just pulled away from the gate and I'd have to notify the lost and found.

Frustrated and baffled, I muttered the words, "Well, this couldn't possibly be any worse."

As soon as those words left my mouth, I felt like a real tool. The kids quickly tuned into my negative, anxious energy and started whining and getting antsy.

Shut up, Jacq. You're supposed to be the example, the person your kids look to in any situation to know that everything is okay.

This is when I shifted my attitude, thanked the man for his help, and decided I'd make the most of being phone-free for the next week.

I was generally with family during our whole trip, so the need to contact anyone never became an issue. But I'll tell you what I didn't do: text Ryan randomly throughout the day, check my Facebook feed, read email and newsletters, browse pictures on Instagram, or tweet random musings.

After a few phoneless days, I noticed something. As I was out at the park, out for dinner, or hanging around the house, I realized just how many people were on their phones all the time. It took me losing my phone to even notice.

While others were staring at their teeny screens — waiting

for something to happen, working, or searching for a dopamine hit — I closed my eyes and tuned into the sights and sounds of what was going on around me. And it felt good.

Turns out, losing my phone led to the greatest part of the weekend. Extra bonding with my kids and my family, who I didn't get to see often after our move to the US. When we lived in Toronto, we'd pop over for dinner on Sunday night, or go out for a meal on a weeknight, whereas now we visit for an entire week or weekend. The time is more focused and intentional when you know you're not going to spend time with these people again for at least a few months. Even better if that time is phone-free.

That phone-free week taught me some essential lessons in smartphone sanity and spurred me to create some new boundaries:

Stop wishing I was somewhere else. I was exactly where I needed to be.

Minimize social media to a few times daily.

Phone-free when hanging out with the kids (this one's still a practice).

Keep the phone out of sight when there's food in front of me (especially now that I'm decidedly un-vegan and rarely take food photos — also, no one cares what's on my plate).

No more checking email first thing in the morning. I move my body, read, or write instead. Often, I'll lay in bed quietly, simply breathing and being present.

No more reading emails, checking the weather, or scrolling Instagram on the toilet.

Now, from time to time, I stay off my phone for a whole weekend and learn a lot about myself and the people around me.

Monday mornings, though, sometimes I find myself back at it. Like a dieter binging on chocolate cake — standing up, at the kitchen counter. Devouring empowerment memes, "Embrace the Flow!" *Oh, I'll need to remember this quote for later!*

I walk into rooms all the time with a purpose and find

myself standing there and wondering what brought me there in the first place. The same is true with social media. Mindlessly, I fire up my phone to "check" if anything is new on Facebook.

And the whole time I'm scrolling, I feel a pull. It's a tiny voice in the back of my mind creating a nagging feeling that I might be wasting time. I have more important things to do — why am I sitting here consuming car selfies, pictures of other people's kids, or photos of perfectly stacked notebooks and candles?

More than money, more than my home, and the few possessions inside, time is my most valuable resource and the one I can control.

Social media is a fantastic tool for connection — and business. Many of the great humans in my life I first met on social media, and the ones I know in real life, I love staying connected with on social media, but how much is too much?

Social media is also a boredom cure, bathroom buddy (oh, c'mon, you know you do it), and creativity killer. When I spend more time consuming than creating and consume before I write a thing, I do not enjoy the human I turn into.

Social media is also where comparison-itis can creep in. It's just as ridiculous to compare yourself to someone on social media as it is to compare yourself to a department store mannequin. Completely constructed, curated, and not always the full truth.

Taking a sip of comparison tea before diving into your important work for the day can leave you doubting yourself. Bring a dose of doubt to your work and guess how effective your work will be? At best, it'll feel watered down, and at worst, it could leave you feeling empty.

When I realized I was scrolling through pages and pages of updates without actually even reading anything, I knew something had to give.

There are apps you can install on your phone and computer

to track your social media usage, and even remove your social feeds altogether — leaving just an inspirational quote.

Calculate how much time you spend on social media in a day. This might be frightening, and maybe you're afraid to — you don't want to know. Try timing yourself just for one day. The act of timing yourself alone will probably light a blowtorch to how much time you're spending on there.

Out of curiosity, I whipped out my calculator to see how much time I'd spend on social media by the time I was a hundred, assuming I live that long.

For simplicity's sake, I estimated spending an hour a day or more on most days. If I've been on social media since 2007 and I spend an hour a day until I'm a hundred, that adds up to 26,645 hours of my life — more than three years.

Three years of looking at pictures and reading about other people's lives.

I thought about what I could accomplish in three years. I could write three books, a hundred blog posts, master a new language, or read fifty books. This book alone took three years — what if I didn't write this book?

Three freaking years. Let that sink in.

Three years scrolling. Three years of thumb flicking. That's enough to give you the worst case of carpal tunnel.

During the time I invested working on this book, I took some intentional breaks from social media — months at a time even. Except for checking on my community and private messages once a day.

Social media needs to serve a purpose for me. I follow accounts that make me feel expansive and push me to become the next best version of myself. For now, I feel good about a few minutes here and there. The trick is to turn my phone to airplane mode in the evening and keep it off until I've at least had my coffee. No special apps or timers, I'm not into being super-strict and rigid — too fussy for me.

Take a look at all of your social media use. Which platforms do you enjoy most? When you're scrolling, does Facebook give you a sense of connection? Does Twitter make you feel angry? When you look at all the pictures on Pinterest, do you feel like you'll never be good enough? Like your home will never be Pinterest-worthy? Do you love looking at pretty photos on Instagram? Or do you feel shitty when you sign off?

If social media makes you feel like shit, then quit. At the very least, curate the hell out of what you let into your precious consciousness.

There are many ways to be mindful of how much you consume.

Create before you consume is one of my favorites. If you roll out of bed, and the first thing you do is fire up the news, you've already lost the day.

The connection should feel good.

Consider just how much time you're spending on there. Not just for the sake of your focus and your productivity, but the people around you. I use social media mainly for business and keeping in touch with family and friends, and yet there's still a need for balance. How available do you want to be to potential clients, your fans, and readers?

If I was spending three years of my life staring at a screen, that's three years of my kids' lives too. Now, that seems completely unfair to do to them. Sorry kids, mommy's got years of social media time to log by the time she dies — assuming I live to a ripe old age.

My friend Vicki McLeod wrote a book on this topic, called *#UNTRENDING: A Field Guide to Social Media that Matters*. When you step away from social media and step back into your life, you're moving down on the list of trending topics, or better yet, you have no idea what those trending topics are anymore. In her book, she asks, "What if your last tweet, post, or otherwise was your last?"

What if you died after your last post? Would you be happy with your last words? Would you have been ranting about traffic or complaining about the weather? Or would you have been sharing joy? Perhaps sharing a story that could drive and create new connections and opportunities for growth. Treat every social media post like it's your last.

Because it very well might be.

Being okay with messy me

It's all smoke and mirrors. That perfect image you're trying to maintain or somehow create.

We show up in makeup with freshly styled hair when all we really wanted to do was roll out in our mascara-free, get-shit-done face and yoga pants.

Why the facade? Why the fakeness? If we're all walking around being fake — how do we know what's real?

Somehow becoming real has become basic.

Basic.

The desire to show up perfectly in all areas of our life is stronger than ever. We see these perfectly polished people in magazines, on TV, and on the internet with their shiny teeth, glowing skin, and the perfect butts and want in on some of that flawlessness.

Except that it's an illusion. All of it. Smoke and mirrors. It's all the product of hours and hours with makeup teams and lighting and airbrushing and a small army of people that know how to make things *appear* perfect.

The kicker — everyone is so worried about showing up perfect for their corner of the world that they're not even noticing that you're less than perfect anyway.

I read a magazine piece a while back about why we need to gather around the table for more meals and conversations: Screen-free, analog time, face-to-face. In the article, the author nodded to the exposed pipes that were on display in his kitchen for months. And it didn't matter; he still had people over.

In our last home, it took a few years to get around to painting over the ugly navy blue trim, so I felt the need to apologize anytime anyone came over. We also had ugly '70s-era paneling in the living room, a closed-off kitchen that made social gatherings awkward, and unfinished floor transitions because we ran out of money when other emergency repair costs went through the roof.

For these reasons, I didn't want to have anyone over or host dinners — it was always too much work. And my house wasn't perfect. "Let's just go out," I'd often suggest.

But you know what? I don't even want a perfect house, if there is such a thing. Have you ever been to someone's home and had them follow you around with a microfiber cloth wiping the fingerprints you just left on their stainless steel fridge or straightening the towel you just used to dry your hands off the bathroom? I have, and it's uncomfortable as hell. I felt like an inconvenience in their home, and I worried about leaving a mess behind. I felt like an unwelcome invader — so I stopped visiting.

I promise if you visit my home, it won't be perfect. I also promise to never follow you around my house with anything that resembles a cleaning device. I might follow you around with a bottle of wine to top off your glass, though.

When you step out from behind the curtain and drop the facade, you realize everyone else is more like you than not. Everyone is worried about what everyone else will think.

Until you drop the act and start showing up and saying, *This is me, I'm awkward, and it's awesome.*

Maybe take the lead and be the first person to do it. If people follow your lead, cool. They might just watch from afar, wishing they were as brave as you. And someday they might be, and you'll be the one who inspired them.

When going live on Facebook and Instagram began to take off, I felt a pang of jealousy and also fear. I was deathly afraid of going on video — especially live. I had stood in front of many rooms and given presentations for my corporate job, but every time I stood up and got ready to open my mouth, panic would bubble up. While I wanted to hurl right there on the floor, I didn't. And it always turned out okay in the end. No one died, and no one puked.

As a business owner, showing up fully has always been important to me, and video was a way I could add dimension. When talking with some other entrepreneurs about going on live video, I said I was scared to show off my man voice. (Our voice always sounds weirder to us than it does to the rest of the world.)

After a bit of prodding from some others to go out and do it — I did it! Was it perfect? Absolutely not. I started small. I wanted to be polished and perfect. I couldn't just show up and record some quick videos without perfect lighting, making sure I had makeup on and my hair done. I only now see the irony.

I started with really short bursts and tried not to think about it too much. First, I recorded some quick videos of our backyard chickens and added my voice to the soundtrack. Then I posted it without stopping to think — overthinking leads to little action. No one told me they hated my voice. And also, I didn't die.

Then, while writing the shitty first draft of this book, I aimed to give regular updates throughout the writing process — sometimes a few times a day. This was when I recorded my face on video for the first time to publish on social media. I was scared, and I recorded the first one three times before I found the guts to post it. I froze. I was completely overthinking it — I wanted to say the right thing to sound perfect, to sound like I was smart and knew what I was doing.

I got tired of overthinking and eventually just blurted some shit out — I have no idea what it was now — and shared it before I could change my mind. This was interesting — when I quiet my mind, something else takes over. Intuition, my gut, a higher power? Whatever you call it, it was a feeling inside, a knowing. I trusted myself to let go and let my gut take the wheel.

I got over my fear of trying to show up perfectly in video, and people started responding. Yes, I recognize that it's validation, but people were joining in the conversation, and I was just the one to start it. I even did a few videos without makeup on — a big step for me.

When I first started my plant-based food blog, I wanted to show up like I knew what I was doing, so I blogged every single day for weeks and only shared the link to my website when I had several articles published. I didn't want anyone to visit my website and see one piddly article. I wanted to show up like I had my shit together.

Now, I give my clients the opposite advice. They ask me when they should publish their blog and wonder how many posts they need. My answer today is *one* — one blog post is all you need to publish a blog. Then show up and write again next week and publish another one. Miss a week? No biggie, post again when you have something useful to share.

My clients sometimes have a lot of fear around publishing their thoughts, and I get it because I used to feel that way too. I do try not to put out entirely half-assed crap into the world — the world has more than enough of that. I put a little thought into it, but don't overthink it — it's a fine line to walk. There's a lot to unpack in there — being seen, doing things we don't normally do, procrastinating, and perfectionism.

Occasionally people tell me about spelling errors in my blog posts or an unfinished email title or a half-baked thought in one of my newsletters. Sometimes they tell me about it publicly, and I roll my eyes and type a quick "thanks!" If it's a big enough mistake, I'll fix it. If not, I'll leave it.

The only way to bust through perfectionism is to keep moving — keep creating. Ignore the smoke and mirrors of others in your industry and stay in your lane.

For this reason, I mostly ignore other writers who talk about similar topics. I try not to pay attention to what kinds of projects they're working on. If they need help, I always try to serve generously. Generally, though, I'm ignoring them, in the kindest Canadian way I can.

I don't want to let all the things other people are creating influence me into thinking I need to be doing something different or that what I'm doing isn't good enough. I want to create deliberately. Put stuff out into the world, help people write better, and get back to work.

Focusing on others in your own industry can also tend to make us take on a voice like our industry peers — and in our messaging and marketing, we end up worrying about impressing our peers, not the people who need to hear from us the most.

It doesn't matter, though. When you start saying, "Hey world, here are all my imperfections — take them or leave them," something changes. Things just get easier. You don't have to pretend anymore — you can just put the baggage down and have a seat.

A different kind of diet

The food kind of diet, well, it's never really been my jam. But years ago, I went on a news diet. I stopped mindlessly listening to the news while doing things around the house. When I did engage, I asked myself if that tidbit of news changed my day or my life in any way. Did I act any differently? Did I really need to know this?

Drink cranberry juice daily to avoid a uterine infection!
Don't hold your cell phone to your ear!
Stop using all plastic!

Mindlessly, I'd flip on the TV right after getting out of the shower, turn on the morning local news, and it would play in the background while I got ready for work, and Ryan and I would watch it while eating bagels or drinking smoothies at the breakfast counter.

The news has a purpose: to inform and educate. But after a while, watching the news feels so terribly hard. How much is too much?

Today, I don't have cable, only a shared Netflix subscription. When the kids and I are out and about and they see the news, often playing in a hotel lobby or while flipping channels at the home of someone who has cable, they always stop and watch —

like the sun, you know you're not supposed to look but you just can't help it. Because the news is seldom on in our home (we'll flip it on for big world events sometimes) — they *love* watching it. We tune into the news intentionally and mindfully now. We'll watch a few different stations and pause to discuss what's happening and answer the kids' questions.

On one particular morning, after the 2016 Orlando nightclub shooting, Jacob and I were traveling for hockey camp, and he was engrossed in the news playing in the hotel breakfast room. He barely touched his scrambled eggs and waffles from the buffet. He had tons of questions. I answered his many questions on the way to the rink (and again later over dinner). Had we been at home, he wouldn't have heard about it from the news. Instead, if we discover a story we believe the kids would benefit from discussing, we tell them the facts, look for lessons, and answer questions.

In the situation of a nightclub shooting, it's not something the kids need to know about — they don't go to nightclubs. So a morning at home would have been relaxing, with egg sandwiches and maybe some cartoons on the TV if it was the weekend.

So, where do we draw the line between staying informed today and complete ignorance? We need to pay attention and throttle our focus so that consuming news stories isn't all we do. Consuming anything without action hurts more than it helps.

In the information age, information isn't always power; it can be overwhelming. It can also be empowering and inspiring. We need to set up filters and learn how to let through only the stuff we need. We get to choose what we take in.

I used to watch both the morning and the evening news, you know, to stay up-to-date on world happenings, on the off chance I felt I needed to sound smart in a group conversation. I've now come to accept that responding, "I didn't hear about that. What happened?" is a perfectly suitable response, and I haven't lost any friends over asking questions like this.

Early 2020 was a different story though. With a flip of a switch, school closed until further notice, along with all but the essential businesses. Watching the news again felt important. We needed to know what was going on.

We dove in with our full attention, devouring every possible story about the virus. We thought about it, we saw evidence of it, we felt it everywhere. Wear a mask, don't wear a mask. Order takeout and support local businesses, but not the delivery service, and you must disinfect everything. Keep your packages outside for three days before bringing them inside. This was the first time we intentionally turned on the news at home. We watched a few different stations to get information on what was happening. Then we spent the next few days answering questions and wiping away tears. Talia would go to bed each night asking if her tiny cough was the virus. She was so full of worry she'd be hysterical with tears. We'd spend an hour every night at bedtime trying to ease her mind so she could rest.

We had just moved into our new home in February 2020, the kids excitedly and tentatively headed to new schools, and just two weeks later, the school doors would close and remained shut through the end of the school year.

Just two days after the kids' school closed, I was going about my business and staying home (which is easy for me as an introvert). Our first Saturday of isolating was a regular day. All sports were canceled, no more birthday parties to attend. I usually don't work on the weekends, but I went about my business puttering around the house. Then, as the sun went down, it got quiet inside, and I fell down the rabbit hole.

The rabbit hole that's Facebook.

Living in a new neighborhood, with new neighbors and new schools, I felt incredibly isolated. I wondered what was going on in my new community, not really feeling like part of it yet. I was craving connection and knowing I couldn't go get it.

I don't know how much time went by, but my best guess is that I probably spent a solid four hours scrolling. I went down neighborhood rabbit holes — community posts, conversations, and comments.

I saw friends' photos of empty toilet paper shelves and empty freezers at grocery stores all over the world.

That's when the pain in my chest started vying for my attention. The last things I googled before going to bed that first Saturday were, "Is 39 too young to have a heart attack?" "chest tightness and coronavirus" and "coronavirus symptoms."

This wasn't a good way to end my day — or spend any time really. This was exactly the reason I didn't endlessly consume the news because I feel it in my body. The next few days, I'd be going about my business and noticing that tightness and heaviness at the top of my chest.

It was my body reacting to stress. I didn't necessarily feel more stressed than anyone else, but because I was listening to others — seeing the photos, posts, comments, and panic-ridden headlines — my body was like, screw you, you can't do this.

I chalked it all up to stress and continued to go through my day, making sure the kids had what they needed for distance learning and giving myself plenty of time-outs to breathe, relax, and unplug.

A few days later at dinner, I started to feel kind of sick. I finished eating and went to lay down on the couch. While lying there, I noticed that my pulse was racing. I only drink one cup of coffee each morning (maybe two on occasion), so I wasn't over-caffeinated, and it was evening.

I felt my heart pounding through my chest and tried figuring out my pulse rate so that I could Google a normal resting heart rate.

Realizing I couldn't simultaneously work a timer on my phone and check my pulse, I asked Ryan to check it for me. He pulled up a timer on his phone, put two fingers on my wrist, and got quiet so he could focus and count.

The kids noticed what was happening, immediately stopped in their tracks, and looked at me — faces blank and concerned.

"Mom, what's wrong?"
"Mom, what are you doing?"
"Dad, why are you doing that?"
"Dad, what's wrong with Mom?"

I felt their panic further mine, which didn't help me. And then I had to make a decision. I had to choose between wearing my strong face for them and pretending like I had it all together, or I could tell them what was going on — calmly and frankly.

So I told them. "My heart feels like it's beating fast, so Daddy's checking it. That's all."

They still wore slightly blank faces, and I reassured them again that I was fine.

That night, I had a dream. I don't recall the exact situation, but I remember the knowing feeling when I woke up. The knowing I had was this…

I'm dying. What am I gonna do?

I woke up feeling heavy, and that was the last day of watching the news for hours without a time limit and a focus. I needed to look after myself first before I could consume news and discuss it with the kids. Because if I'm not grounded, clear, rested, and healthy, that's not going to support anyone else.

This was a wake-up call about all the things that are unsustainable. Letting my needs and wants slide to the bottom of the list will only work for so long. Consuming news to the point of overdose will make me sick.

What I didn't want the kids to remember about this time was Mommy sprawling on the couch, unable to look after myself after watching the news.

During our adventures in social distancing, the kids aren't gonna remember the school assignments, what they ate for dinner, or what they saw on the news. They will remember how we handled the news, how we respond to crisis, how to communicate our needs and learn how to share theirs.

Just like during any other period, you can hit that magical unsubscribe, unfollow, or delete button when it's too much. I received an email from every restaurant mailing list I've ever joined telling me that their restaurant was clean. *Well, that's good to know.*

Doing this frees up a ton of time and energy. I direct my thoughts elsewhere where I can do something. It's easy to become obsessed with information. Do you need to check the exact number of virus cases in your state or your country several times a day? Why do we have this uncontrollable need to be the first to know the latest news and for what? To impress our friends? To be the first of a dozen of us sharing the exact same news article on Facebook? Do you need to know all the details of the debates about how your child's school will handle online learning? Or do you just need to know when they have a plan in place so you can find out what it is?

If you've never tried a news diet, try it for just a day. Part of your job may require you to stay on top of certain news. I get it, I've been there. If that's the case, keep it at that. Outside of your career, turn off the news channels. If you need to know what's happening in the world, ask someone you trust what's important to know. They'll tell you, and then you can choose to consciously consume information. Turn it on, gather what you need to know, then turn it off.

Without four hours a day on the news, what will you do with that time instead? Maybe you'll talk to more people and have some inspiring conversations. Perhaps you'll spark new connections. Talk to human beings, face-to-face and on the phone. Read more books, magazines, or newspapers. We take in information differently when it's in our hands.

Perhaps you'll spend that time dedicated to a big project. That idea you've been dreaming about for years.

The busy trap

If you know me, you've probably never heard me use a particular dirty four-letter word to describe my time or lack thereof — busy.

As a natural-born people-pleaser, the oldest sibling, and a woman, I grew up wanting to make everyone happy all the time — especially my parents. I focused on getting good grades, being "nice," and being an all-around good human being. I was the kid that would feel devastated when someone said they were disappointed in me.

I tried to make my teachers happy — friends often called me a teacher's pet, which led me to want to make my friends happy, so I'd strategically act up in class to show them that I had their backs too. I'd also spend time helping them with homework and doing more than my fair share on group projects.

People-pleasing runs deep, and when we say yes to everyone, there's no time left for us, which leads us to feel (and complain about being) busy.

Busy is a choice. We fill our day with things to do by choice. It's easy to say, "But I don't have a choice." I always have a choice.

It might be the overuse of the term "busy" that sounds like

nails on a chalkboard. Busy is also a relative description of time. I can't tell you I'm busier than you. We're both "busy," doing stuff, running around to different activities.

How have you been?

Busy.

I got so sick of hearing myself say this. It felt so boring, so mediocre.

Well, no shit, aren't we all? That's no way to describe all the cool stuff I've been up to. I'm doing great work in the world, and if I simply sum it up as "busy," I'm doing myself a huge disservice. There's no prize at the end of my life for being the busiest, so why was I wearing it like a badge of honor?

If I get to the end of my life and realize I was too busy to enjoy it, running around from obligation to obligation, then who won the race?

We use the word "busy" to validate our existence — even if we don't want to admit it. I know because that was me. I was important. Look at me; I'm so busy over here. I have a full calendar, so I must be successful. And no time to think about how I might not actually be so successful. And for good measure, I must make sure everyone knows how busy I am so they can see how important I am too.

If I'm busy at work, does this mean I have a successful career?

If my home life is busy, then I must be fulfilled, right?

If my social life is busy, does that mean I have great friends?

Busy is no way to describe a life. It's a lazy way to talk about our work and daily activities. I decided to scrap the word from my vocabulary and get specific. My life is full — with tasks and experiences. My job is to figure out which experiences fulfill me, and then choose more of those.

If you haven't guessed by now, I'm not perfect, and I catch myself rushing through things sometimes — especially my less than favorite stuff like laundry, dishes, or helping the kids with Common Core math homework so I can move on and get to the next task. Maybe it's a task that I'll enjoy just a little bit more, so I feel busy, busy, busy.

First, I needed to unbusy myself. When I was in my corporate job, I couldn't simply remove a bunch of meetings from my calendar. What I *could* do was block some extra time on my calendar each day so that others wouldn't snatch up all my availability. I scanned my schedule for upcoming appointments that felt like obligations and backed out of what I could. No one missed me, and I carved out more time for myself.

One glance at my calendar and I could quickly tell the things that I secretly (or even not so secretly) wished I could get out of. That feeling means that I should have politely declined in the first place.

When you start saying no more often, you might worry that people aren't going to like you anymore. You're going to lose all your friends, and you're going to be a lonely cat lady who plays solitaire all day and waits for the mailman so you can complain if they're an hour "late." Don't be a crazy lonely cat lady. Unless, of course, you want to be.

Start by cleaning out your calendar. What's coming up in the next week that you wish you'd said no to? Ask yourself if you can get out of it. If you can — do it! You can back out gracefully.

Tell them you took on more than you could handle this week, and you need to decline.

If it's a party, say you can't make it.

And remember that "no" is a complete sentence.

As much as you feel the need to explain to protect people's feelings, I can assure you that people care much less than you think they do. They're often worried about their own obligations and even their people-pleasing habits.

Once you've cleared some space on your calendar, leave it there. Go ahead and block it off, if you like, so that you know you'll have your free time. Then protect it like a motha. When the time block arrives, you might wonder what to do with it.

Keep a list of things you enjoy, save it for the inevitable surprise stuff, or do nothing at all.

Now that you've created some space on your calendar, you can stop saying you're busy. First, we all are, and second, no one gives a crap. They're tired of your lame-ass excuses, and you're probably tired of using them.

Instead of complaining about your never-ending busy-ness, try these on:

How are you?

I'm filling my time these days with lots of exciting things! Editing my book, building an empire — you know, the regular stuff.

Nice to see you, what's new?

I've been writing like a MOFO and running the kids around to hockey, gymnastics, karate, and piano.

Also, saying you're "busy but good" doesn't count. This is lazy communication. Instead, try using your answer to the question "How was your weekend?" as an opportunity to open up and connect, sharing more about yourself and your personal life. If people seem uninterested, who cares? (Well, obviously not them) But don't let it stop you — it's on them, not on you. Simply describe what you're actually doing. It's easy to keep people at arm's length, but when you take the time to open up and let people into your world a little, you're fostering a connection.

Be the example. You might inspire someone listening to open up and share a little more the next time they feel the urge to sum up their lives with, "busy."

Also, your kids are listening (if you have them). How excited do you think they will be to grow up if growing up means that they're going to be busy (and complaining about it) all the time? Being a grown-up sounds pretty sucky in this case.

I'm diligent about creating space for the kids too. If one of them is whining about an activity after a week, maybe it's time to take a break or quit. When we can reschedule, I give them the option to say no, even if it's just to stay home (except for hockey because that shit is expensive — kidding!). Giving kids some control over their schedule and empowering them to make decisions will serve them later.

Saying you're filling their schedule to keep them out of trouble is a recipe for burnout. How would you feel if you never had time to binge-watch Netflix or enjoy a big glass of wine or read a book for an afternoon, just for fun?

I want to create conscious kids who can make decisions and choose when they need a change — kids that can listen to their guts when we give them the opportunity.

Let's measure our success by something other than how much we accomplished in a day.

Also, you've done enough for today.

Rest is a verb

"I'm so sick of doing the same thing every day."

I say this a lot.

The kids used to say it every Wednesday, when they'd be sick of coming home from school, feeding the dog, eating dinner, doing homework, and running the bedtime gauntlet — shower, book, and bed. I can't say I blame them. I feel the strain of monotony sometimes.

It's that tedious nagging when I'm at the sink, simultaneously making dinner, washing dishes, feeding the dog, and maybe listening to a business audiobook.

Over and over, it's like I'm living a real-life version of Groundhog Day. I eat the same thing for breakfast every day — which is a good way to save your brainpower for bigger and more important things, but sometimes, it all starts to look and feel the same. And that sameness can wear on you.

At first, I wondered if it was boredom. But digging deeper, it might not be a boredom problem after all. It could be FOMO (the fear of missing out) or something else. *Am I only bored because I think my friends are all out there having more fun than me and doing way cooler things?* Maybe it's because I've been watching curated lives on Instagram.

When those waves of ennui set in, I need to figure out if it's something I need to change. And, if so, am I even ready for it? What's behind this awkward, tedious feeling?

There are two things I do when I feel stuck:

(1) Embrace it.

(2) Change it.

Routine and mediocrity can be perfectly acceptable. Most of our lives are mundane, repetitive, and so very ordinary. And if you think celebrities' and moguls' lives are more exciting than yours, look a little closer and you'll probably see that these people do boring-ass shit like grocery shopping every Sunday night or wearing the same three outfits on rotation just like us.

You're the same people.

It's in these quiet and mundane moments of our lives where, if you can shift to accepting and even embracing them, you'll find the most magic.

It's when I can pause, take a step back, and look at the big picture. Standing at the kitchen sink, feeling my bare feet on a cushioned mat, and seeing my family — safe, comfortable, not a single apparent worry. Those are the moments when I know this is where I'm supposed to be.

And then I can join them in that well-loved spot on the couch and simply sit.

But when I simply sit, why do I feel guilty, as if I'm not being productive? Why is it so hard to do nothing? To just sit and be? I'm probably not the first to tell you that you're a human *being* and not a human *doing*.

In school, if you were caught doing nothing — or worse, tried to explain yourself and told your teachers there was a method to your fuckery — you would have been promptly booted from class and sent to the principal's office.

Why are kids so good at doing nothing? Is it because they simply don't give a shit about our busy badges of honor? Because for a kid to say they are too busy to play is a serious offense.

Imagine a sixth-grader saying, "Sorry, dude. I was so busy

last weekend. I didn't have a single second to log in to Xbox." This would be met with raised eyebrows and, "Oh, that sucks, I'm so sorry."

When I was a kid, I remember entire weekends when I didn't leave the house. I also wasn't part of the popular crowd — if I didn't have weekend plans, I'd easily fritter away a whole weekend with nothing. I'd sit and draw or listen to music for hours, recording my favorite songs on a cassette tape.

No one gave me shit for not accomplishing enough or not learning or growing.

I need to know — when did it start to matter? When did my doing nothing make me less than?

On the one hand, there's something in ourselves that craves change, so we have to do something. Taking a step, learning, changing are all actions.

Perhaps doing nothing is an excellent way to create a change — in our minds, in the speed we hurl through life, and in an effort to be awake to this ride. Yet in our online world where we get likes and shares for all the stuff we make, buy, and accomplish, how can we celebrate stillness?

Imagine reading this post in your social feed:

I did absolutely fucking nothing today. I didn't even cook my own food. I stared at the sky, I picked my belly button lint, and lint from a few other random places I didn't even know could collect it. I lay on the couch with the TV off and all my books closed and just stared at the ceiling for a while, then closed my eyes for a bit longer. I didn't even nap. I have no idea how long I did this for. And it was fantastic.

Maybe your first thoughts would be "Fucking slacker" or "It must be nice."

Flash forward to the spring of 2020 and with the news of the coronavirus sending everyone into their homes to stay, there were lots of days (and weeks and months, depending on where you live) that looked like this. We were all slackers, though many of us went into shelter-in-place with big goals.

At first, I was excited.

All this time at home without school drop-offs and pick-ups, hockey, gymnastics, dance, and piano.

I'm going to have so much free time!

With the flip of a switch as soon as school was canceled here, life changed. I thought to myself, "I'll finally finish my book revisions," "I'll be able to write so much," "My website will finally get all the updates it needs," "There are so many things on my to-do list I'll be able to do."

I can *do* so much more. I can show up and *do* more.

And I wonder why my mind immediately went to being productive.

Why did I feel the need to be so productive? Why wasn't I excited for rest?

Sometimes change is slow and deliberate, and other times, it's hurled at you like a twenty-pound medicine ball. You either brace your gut, stretch out your arms, and catch it or get the hell out of the way and hope you don't smash your toes.

Yes, we saw this change coming, but until it's in your backyard and on everyone's lips, it's not reality.

In one day, we went from a calendar full of activities, a full day of school, a full day of work, to our new routine of sheltering in place.

There was life before social distancing and life after. Life before was filled with days stuffed full like an extra ten pounds of chocolate cake stuffed into a crisp, brand new pair of Spanx. Anything we thought we might have room for — *sure, stuff it in*. It'll fit, just push harder. Anything we were afraid to say no to — *sure, we'll figure it out*.

And yes, I can schedule the kids' activities to start within ten minutes of each other when they're a twenty-minute drive away. I'll just leave earlier.

Holy shit. Just reading about pre-March 2020 life is fucking exhausting.

Week one of adjusting to the crisis was also jam-packed.

Let's see how many calls I can squeeze in. If we're going to be home all week, we need some more groceries, toilet paper, and wine. I can do more than I did last week, I'll have all the time in the world.

I hosted a few extra coaching sessions for clients and revised copy for clients who needed to pivot.

Day one of the kids' distance learning, they were done with "school" by 11:00 a.m. Yet I was plugging away and looked up at the clock: 6:00 p.m. Holy crap — normally the bulk of my workday would end at 3:00 p.m. when I'd get the kids from school. And now, well, I could be more productive.

I probably don't need to tell you this, but this sprint didn't last long. By Thursday of week one, I was laying on the couch after dinner checking my pulse and Googling normal pulse rates.

Everything slowed down. The tightness in my chest and a sore throat forced me to hit the brakes. I wasn't going to try and muscle my way through. We could have weeks, maybe months at home like this, and this pace was not sustainable. I was fine, it was just stress.

Heck, our lives before were unsustainable — and look what happened.

Work, activities, school, family, the speed at which we could get grocery bags filled with foods we can't pronounce from far-off lands, but you know, we *need* them — all unsustainable.

In the first week of the change, I was sleeping between nine and eleven hours each night. I set my alarm for a little later and still went to bed by 10:00 p.m. Why was I so exhausted? Because that seven-minute mile pace I'd been running in my life wasn't working for me anymore. Sure, my business grew more in 2019 than it did in 2018 — but was I any happier? Were all my big projects getting finished? Slow progress and lots of stops and starts most of the way around.

I was forced to get more intentional with how I spent every minute. Instead of filling my day with stuff that didn't matter, it stared me in the face.

What urgently mattered for me was managing my energy, looking after my health, helping my family look after theirs, finding more work and play that lights me up, resting, and raising resilient, kind, and healthy kids.

We had many hints up until this time that it was time to slow down. During a busy winter season, there were days when the kids, fed up with their packed schedule, would ask, "Can we just stay home?" They were feeling it too. And all they wanted to do was stay in their pj's, play video games, or run around outside.

We had oscillated from doing less to doing more and found ourselves overscheduled every single day with an activity. Because what the heck would happen if our kids didn't have somewhere to be every day of the week?

Much of it, we wouldn't trade, and neither would the kids. Do they need to be engaged in two, even three, different activities a season? What if they even found themselves bored and had to entertain themselves? What could they create then? What if we could drop the urgency to feel productive, having to do *something*?

Then what?

We've come to believe that we have to do something to be something.

Yes, we have some shit to do, and there are do-ers who we needed to *do* right now more than ever. But when it comes to the busy work and the breakneck pace of life, it's time to *be* more than it is to *do*. Yet another reminder. When will we get it?

Sit around doing nothing for too long, and maybe your partner or kids walk in, see you there doing nothing, like a psycho, and ask if you're sick. Maybe they poke you in the arm to see if you're still breathing. Because God knows that's the only time you've slowed down at all in the last eight years. It takes a world shake-up to knock you on your ass.

If you've turned off the news, limited social media, cut out the energy vampires, and left the circus, what's left to do with your time? You might have time to rest now. Imagine that resting, sleeping, daydreaming, and doing nothing at all could help you actually get further, faster. Doing nothing is good for my mood, my energy, and my creativity. So why is it so hard?

Leave some blank space on my calendar, and I'll find a way to fill it. Even when I schedule "do nothing" time, it feels incredibly dull, and I resist it. How will I grow my business? How will I learn the new skills I want to learn? How will I achieve a new level of success by doing nothing?

The whole point is to get my body and mind out of the addiction to the go-go-go mode and start to accept the slow-the-fuck-down mode. Because it's in those slow moments that I recharge my batteries and sometimes get my biggest intuitive hits and inspiration.

It's odd to me that we crave instructions and a step-by-step guide to doing nothing, but I get it. When I've been moving through my day at the speed of light without taking a breath, I might plop down on the couch and feel a pull to do something — write something, wipe the counter, fold the laundry, walk the dog. And I don't want to.

Goof off, turn my email off, unplug, let it sit for a couple of seconds before I begin again. You know, pretty much the same process I'd follow if my computer wasn't working.

This *is* the work. Finding stillness, silence, and surrender within the madness.

When was the last time you lit a candle and watched the flame? If you can light a big mother bonfire in your backyard, do that instead — I promise it'll be much more inspiring. In the absence of a bonfire, though, a candle will do.

Journaling just for shits and giggles, with the only goal of moving your hand. Painting a canvas only to feel the brush soak in acrylic color and swirl it around. Not to turn it into something you can hang in a gallery or prop up on your fireplace mantle.

Because out of the quietness and stillness of nothing is where ideas happen. It's where complicated problems get stupidly simple solutions.

Doing nothing can solve problems. Not that I want you to think about it that way. But when you create on-demand and are expected to produce brilliance at a moment's notice, practicing doing nothing is going to make you more creative and more amazing, not less. I know you didn't think it was even possible, did you?

The year 2020 taught me what was most important. It made me revisit my life values and ask myself, am I really living them? If health is number one, why am I working so many hours and watching news on repeat?

This giant pause button was another reminder for me to keep slowing down. Question everything and cut out all the bullshit.

FOMO is a bitch

FOMO, or the fear of missing out, is the worry that deep down, we're not doing what we're supposed to be, whether in that moment or with all our life minutes. It's what can keep me from enjoying a conversation with a new acquaintance at a party because I'm worried that I should be talking to someone different or that I'm spending too much time with one person.

It's the absolute worst at events where I hardly know a soul. Where do I start? Am I having lunch at the table that's going to offer inspiring conversation or will I wind up with the energy vampires? Should I have paired up with someone to share a hotel room so I'd get to know them better rather than prioritizing my introvert time?

Definitely a no on that last one.

FOMO prevents me from fully enjoying a moment because there might be another moment I feel I "should" be soaking up. The biggest problem with living in FOMO-mode is that you can never enjoy the present moment if you're overly concerned with the next one, or what could be going on in the next room or two conversations over.

That fear of missing something is the root cause of saying yes to all the things. I used to say yes to projects, get-togethers, and bake sales (and I hate baking) because I was afraid to say no. Unfortunately, those things I said yes to didn't magically turn into exciting events. They became obligations. And then my schedule was full of a bunch of shit I didn't want to do in the first place.

When my calendar was full of obligations it was a calendar full of fear.

When I worked in corporate, there was pressure to say yes to everything — that's what they were paying me for. When I was focused on getting out of corporate on my terms, I started turning down the extra projects, happy hours, and events in favor of putting my priorities back on the calendar.

It's been an effort for me to pause before committing. Especially since people-pleasing is my standard operating mode, and nothing makes me happier than seeing people I care about happy. Now, when a new opportunity lands in my inbox, I pause and let it sit for at least a day before responding. For me, if it's not a *hell yes*, it's a hell no. But because I'm Canadian, it's *no thank you*, and *thanks for understanding.*

Sure, I sometimes do things I don't necessarily want to do for family and friends — but even if I'm not overly excited about it, I'm doing it to help out — like writing a eulogy. I wouldn't say I was excited about it, but there was a need, and I could show up, serve, and have a positive impact on others. That feels good for me and is aligned with how I want to feel — which is generally useful.

It happened in my client work too. When I first left my corporate job, I said yes to any and all freelance copywriting work. I threw my name into the hat on so many projects that were just *okay,* but I just wanted to get my hands dirty and give some stuff a try. There's totally a place and time for this. I ended up working with some people that weren't for me and doing some work that felt tedious and maybe a little boring or misaligned, but in some of those moments, it was fear that had me. I was afraid that another writer would come along and take the job, then they'd hire that writer for everything forever and ever, and I'd never be able to get another client ever again. Welcome to the crazy-train inside my brain.

As soon as I shifted to thinking about all the cool projects out there that I *could* work on and all the people I could impact, I started sitting back somewhat and letting work come to me, so to speak. I know, if you're in business, you might think I'm bonkers — that's not how you build a business, by sitting back and letting shit come to you. But it worked, and it worked well.

I planted those seeds, set the intention, and kept moving forward.

What happened when I stopped with the FOMO was that I trusted that the opportunities coming my way were coming to me for a reason. You can still run your business as a professional, and if you trust the right things will come your way if you create space for them, they just might.

Instead of FOMO, leave some open space in all the places in your life. Just like creating space physically by clearing out the crap in your home that you don't need or love. You can think straight and spend less time thinking about your stuff.

Same with your time. Fill it with experiences you care about. Blocking your calendar is another way to create space. That space is for opportunities that feel like a hell yes to your gut.

It means I block my calendar a few days a week, and also for a few weeks every year. People can usually only book calls with me two days a week between noon and 3:00 p.m.

To really open your eyes to the whole FOMO thing, open your favorite social media app and search #fomo. You'll get to read about all the shit people think they're missing. It's wild research.

The only thing I was missing with FOMO was my actual life. It's right in front of me, happening to me right now, and I'm too busy worrying there's something "better" to do. That's a little trick my brain likes to play on me to keep me scared and playing small.

Maybe you're reading this book and having some serious FOMO that there's a better book for you right now. And perhaps there is. If you're not having fun right now or learning something, put this book down and do something else. See, the FOMO could be keeping you reading this book because you're afraid to miss something good like the magical unicorn that appears in the next chapter.

See what I did there?

FOMO makes you finish a book that sucks (hopefully, not this one) or finish a movie that sucks even though you were bored thirty minutes in. You're afraid to miss out on something — a surprise, a wow moment, or a happy ending. If something sucks, move on. If a book isn't grabbing me after a few chapters, I put it down. There are so many more books out there waiting for me.

The next time you're at a party, simply notice your internal FOMO and the FOMO of others. You can see the look of FOMO on someone's face. Maybe you're the poor soul at a party on the other end of someone experiencing FOMO. Notice they're probably looking around the room, half smiling, and you're wondering if they heard a word you're saying. If you think someone's not listening, you can have some fun with them. Throw in "...and then my head blew up," and see if they notice.

If they carry on like nothing happened — excuse yourself. You get to choose to be around people that are also present in their lives — in every conversation.

The secret to having time is protecting it like a MOFO

Time is our most valuable resource because it's not renewable. And it really fucks us up. We're always worried, running around like we don't have enough of it — when really, if we shut up for a few minutes, we'd realize that we got ourselves into this mess in the first place.

There were many times in my life when I felt like I had no control over my time — starting in school. There were school hours, then homework, and sports… The same pattern repeated in college, and eventually in every job. Then I had kids. I honestly can't recall what I did with my time before kids. I sure hope I wasn't one of those kid-less dicks that whined about being busy.

Kids give zero fucks about your time. Bad dream at 2:00 a.m., wet bed at 3:00 a.m. — I've got your number, Mom.

One morning while getting ready for the day, I woke the kids up at 6:00 a.m. to get them to the school's before-care program by 6:30, so I could get to the office by 7:30. I had everything in place like most mornings. Breakfast ready to go so they could eat in the car, my bag packed, everyone's stuff lined up by the door.

Talia was just about three, and her little hands were fussing with her boots. I crouched down, hoping not to tear the seam in my pencil skirt, and she refused my assistance. Independent three-nager as she was, she wasn't going to let me help.

I picked the boots up, threw them against the wall, and screamed, "Put your own fucking boots on," and stormed out to put my bags in the car, giving me some sense of progress.

Pulling myself together, looking up at the sky for strength, I walked back into the house, and what I saw made me cry.

Jacob was crouched down now, calmly and patiently helping Talia with her boots. I backed into the doorway and slid down the wall, not giving a shit if my pencil skirt gave out.

Why was I rushing around and yelling at the kids to go to a job I hated?

This was the moment I got super protective about my time and how I invested every minute of it. I was done with running around like a squirrel all the time.

The reason I was still in a job that I didn't love was that I hadn't focused yet. I didn't yet make the time. And making the time would be the only way to make it happen.

Take this book, for instance. To write it, I made a plan a few weeks before I'd go into head-down writing mode. Then, every day for thirty days, as part of national novel writing month (NaNoWriMo) in November of 2017, I got up at 5:30 a.m., made coffee, sometimes journaled for a few minutes, and then started writing. With a goal of 50,000 words by November 30, I had to write 1,667 words each day. I'd stop when I was done or when I needed to tend to a kid or get them off to school. If I didn't finish my writing for the day in the morning, I'd do it at night. I would go to sleep each day knowing I did what I could, and I was on track.

I shared my progress on social media to keep me accountable. And it helped because I might have dropped this project like a hot potato after three days. Instead, I kept going. The first draft of this chapter comes to you from day twenty-two. Well into my new daily writing habit.

And then, this book sat for a year. I burnt out on the project and was thoroughly sick of it. It sat collecting Google dust until November of 2018 when I picked up my project again and dusted it off for NaNoWriMo 2018. I edited every day that month and then shipped it off to my editor.

I got the edits back early in 2019 and then treated it like a bad boyfriend. I'd spend time with it in bits and spurts, going months without even so much as an affectionate thought.

The first draft of this book was purely self-development: very few stories and all advice. An intuitive I consulted with earlier that year said something about this book that made me rework the entire thing. I told her all about my book, and she said, "Don't hate me, but I think your book is a memoir."

I let that idea sit for months before I even considered it. When I jumped back into this book, reading my editor's comments, it clicked. Oh fuck, this *is* a memoir!

Enter NaNoWriMo 2019, where I turned off social media for thirty days and turned on to the idea of making the time to finally finish this book.

People gasp, "How do you have time to write a book?" I made time. It took less than an hour each day to get the words out. Now, the words weren't pretty when they first came out — the point was only to get them out. Getting a shitty first draft into the world is a huge and necessary first step. After that, I needed to figure out what would come next and how to approach the re-drafting and editing.

I repeatedly needed to prioritize this book in order to finally have these words reach beyond my editor and get to you. I had to keep committing to it.

I made the time to write (and edit, tweak, rework, and market) this book because it was something I gave a shit about. Not writing it was going to piss me off more than anything, so I had to write it. I made the time and made it happen.

For me, it was also about congruence. I'm a freaking writing coach! I need to have at least one big project out in the world to feel aligned with the advice I share with other business owners and aspiring authors.

Now, when you say you don't have time to do something or time to relax or read books or take an online class — is it really that you don't have the time? Or have you not made the time? You haven't made the time because it's not a priority or because you said yes to too many other things. Or you really don't want the thing after all.

Start with micro-commitments. Say no to just a couple things you know will weigh you down and start making the time to do some shit for yourself. Start with just ten minutes a day — a small enough chunk of time that's easy to start and sustain.

Dedicate that ten minutes each day to thinking about your project. I'm not even telling you to do any real work on it yet — sit and think for ten minutes a day for one week. Then try twenty minutes a day the next week, and jot down some notes or look up some resources. Then, block your calendar, and increase that time to thirty or forty minutes a day. Once you get into the habit of doing something every single day, the time will become automatic, meaning you won't need to think about it. You may even come to crave that time. Maybe it's first thing in the morning, right after lunch, or right before dinner. I don't recommend saving it until the end of the day — it will be too easy to skip over and choose sleep if that's the case.

Ever watched a kid engrossed in play? They act like they have all the fucking time in the world — because they do. The only time kids are in a hurry is if they're doing something they don't like to do. They might be in a hurry to get to the end of the school day or in a rush to finish their chores so they can get to more fun things.

All the other times — kids are the best at savoring the moment in front of them. They just don't know this. Ask a ten-year-old to clean their room, and they'll disappear for hours.

Because cleaning means go play with the toys at the bottom of the toy box you forgot you had. Kids don't care what time it is; they have no schedule. They have no obligations, and they sure as shit are experts at saying no.

How can you savor time like a kid by spending it engrossed in your passion project? Start today.

Meditation my way

Meditation and mindfulness — I knew they were good for me but couldn't seem to find the time or space to do them consistently. I know that meditation can change my brain for the better, make me happier, calmer, and smarter, but who gets to say *what kind of meditation and how much* is right for me?

The same goes for getting to the gym, eating less sugar, and growing my savings account.

It took me a decade to find a groove with meditation that works for me. I read the books, followed the advice of gurus, and dutifully checked off a small meditation a day in a guidebook. And yet, I was forcing a meditation habit.

If I don't get interrupted within the first three breaths, that's a mediation miracle. Yes, it's hard. Sitting there with your thoughts, trying not to think all at the same time, and acknowledging your thoughts and letting them float on by — you know, "like a cloud in the sky," they say. There's a lot going on up in here.

We seem to think that meditation has to be this big, grand thing. Before we even start meditating, we need to dedicate a meditation space, buy a meditation pillow, create an altar, make sure the house is quiet, the pets are locked up, everyone is sleeping, and our homes are set to the perfect temperature.

This is a load of mindful crap. The conditions are never going to be perfect.

Just because big-time CEOs and entrepreneurs attribute their success to their twice-daily, sixty-minute meditation, it might not be for you. And that's okay because it wasn't always for me either.

I've mostly given up on "meditation" after trying for more than a decade. Instead, I inject bursts of mindfulness throughout my day. I'm getting all the benefits from stealing little moments throughout the day with a thirteen-minute guided meditation, or a twenty-minute hypnosis now and again. And most of all, I'm feeling calmer about the whole thing.

Closing your eyes and breathing has some positive benefits. Notably, it can help you get in touch with your inner self, learn how to keep calm, and deepen your breathing, which will increase your mental focus and make you more fun to be around. I think wine also does the same thing for me, but you may disagree.

Starting with the second I pop my eyes open, I lay in bed, completely still, scanning my body, simply noticing any sensations, hands over my heart, feeling gratitude — *thank you*. I imagine there's this space behind my heart that radiates light. It lights up my whole bod, the room, and all the people I like.

Small, mindful moments add up over time. Sometimes I try to pay attention when I make my morning coffee. The sound of the spark that lights the gas stove, the warmth of the flame, the smell as the grinder pulverizes the fresh coffee beans. I'm pretty serious about my coffee. All I need to do is to be right there in that moment. And then of course, I enjoy a warm cup of caffeinated goodness. Then, when I lay eyes on my family for the first time of the day, I can be present. Hello, people, you get my full attention.

In the shower, I take my time, feel the water, and enjoy the damn shower — instead of running through my to-do list and forgetting to rinse out the shampoo.

When washing dishes, I just wash the dishes.

Occasionally, when I find myself in the middle of a shit storm or need a time out, I will close my eyes and breathe for a few minutes. No timer, no mediation goal, only quieting the mental chatter.

For me, writing is meditative. Every time I sit down at my desk to work, write, or lead a coaching call, I light a candle, write down something I'm feeling grateful for, and take a few deep, present breaths. Finding stillness and feeling grounded before I even lay my fingers on the keyboard helps the words flow (even if they're utter garbage sometimes.) Writing brings me more peace — emptying the words out of my brain and onto a page makes me a better human. Maybe more than meditating will.

Even the small and seemingly mundane and mindless moments are the best times to steal a moment among the madness.

In the car, if I arrive early at any destination or hear a song I love — I sit and enjoy it, or sometimes belt it out at the top of my lungs (the kids don't like this). When I'm driving, I can practice mindfulness with my eyes open. As I travel along, I focus on breathing. Sit up straight, shoulders back, inhale, exhale, and repeat. It's about being fully present in the moment.

Walking meditation is also a favorite way for me to stay present, walking the dog in the morning, only looking around and noticing. When I get the urge to pick up my phone during every life pause or red light, I can stop and simply be bored. I don't need to fill every second with something — especially the mindless social media scroll. When I'm walking or driving, I don't stuff whatever information or learning I can into the time — podcasts, audiobooks. I can drive, walk, and even run with nothing but the sound of my breath.

I also find that traveling the same old route with the intention of discovering something new that I hadn't seen before helps me when I'm stuck on a problem, searching for a solution, stressed, or need to get up and move from the computer screen. Taking a short walk boosts my creativity and lets me come back to my work or sticky problem with renewed focus.

When I sit down to dinner, even on taco Tuesday, I can take a moment to be grateful, and I'm not the praying kind. Silence the phone, light a candle, sit down, and just enjoy two breaths focusing on my food before I start. I do this all the time, whether I'm alone or in a group. No one will notice or even care. Taking one mindful inhale and exhale, in my head, I say, "thank you," then enjoy my food using all my senses.

In those few quiet moments as I get in bed, I take a few minutes to jot things down in a journal. I write as little or as much as I like. Sometimes it's only a single sentence or a lone word. Sometimes it's four pages. I think about the best things that happened, and imagine how I'll feel the next day, as I lay in bed — it's a fantastic way to set myself up for a great day.

It's a practice in noticing — in other words, paying the fuck attention. It's an exercise in choosing your focus and also not filling every single second with mindless shit. The more you can get out of your head and into where you are at a given moment — I promise people will start to notice a shift in your general level of awesomeness and your ability to create conscious change for yourself.

Let's make a distinction here. Meditation is tuning out the world and focusing on your breathing, or other feelings and sensations. Mindfulness is a mental state we achieve by consciously focusing on something. And finally, daydreaming is imagining something — usually something other than what we're physically doing.

Now that I've made that distinction, I'm going to blow it up and say that maybe daydreaming, doing absolutely nothing, or even riding a motorcycle through the mountains is your meditation, or maybe it's dripping some acrylic on canvas, welding, tinkering, coding — whatever your craft or art form.

There's no need to overthink it or to tell yourself, "I'm going to meditate now" — it's like announcing you're going to the bathroom. Completely unnecessary for anyone over the age of five. Just get up and go to the bathroom. You already have permission.

If the image of a yogi dressed in white, surrounded by crystals, sage, and incense is too much for you — it doesn't need to be that way. That's just that yogi's way of meditation, and it works for them.

You could get all the same benefits from petting your dog or brushing your hair. Any efforts you make at mindfulness don't have to be larger than life.

You can download all the apps, attend all the retreats, whatever you need. But ask yourself — what are you hoping to get out of meditation? Are you trying to be as successful and smart as the next billionaire CEO? Or are you just wanting to stop feeling like a crazy asshole all the time? Because if it's really the latter — the rest of the stuff around mindfulness is just a distraction. The apps, trinkets, and ten (or twelve or twenty) steps are all helping you procrastinate instead of getting to what really matters. You already have everything you need and all the tools. There's no getting it "right" — just right for you.

Spiritual labor

Heart-centered, woo woo, the universe, the muse, the law of attraction, whatever you want to call it — I used to turn my nose up at all of it. Thinking you can make whatever change you want if you just think about it hard enough and keep rattling off positive affirmations is lazy at best. Reaching a goal is one part manifestation, one part getting off your ass and doing the work.

Listen, I'm all for having a purely positive attitude over a crap-ass negative-Nancy one (sorry, Nancy). You can be the most positive Pollyanna in the world, and shit will still challenge you sometimes. You need to want it first, then get out there and make it happen. Action is the difference between dreamers and doers.

There was some bigger power involved in me finally saying goodbye to my corporate job and starting my own business. I had to combine my thinking with action-taking to make things happen, and even then, I needed to let go of the outcome and let it unfold however it wanted to. The cool part is that when you surrender, you might get something even better than you had imagined.

When I wanted to turn my side business into a full-time

income, I got up most days at 5:00 a.m. to work on it. I spent many nights sitting on the couch, building my business, finding clients, writing blogs, and tweaking my website. I didn't just sit around at my cubicle every day wishing that I'd leave my job, but I did play some mind tricks while taking serious action.

Every morning I'd get out of bed and pretend I was getting ready to start my day as a full-time freelancer and not as corporate employee #2,678. I'd shower with a smile, looking forward to my day that I was about to spend sitting in my home office, just off the kitchen, looking out the window at the trees. I steeped in the positive feelings that being my own boss would bring. In reality, I was going to sit in the car for over an hour and drive to a sad, gray office overlooking concrete. I also changed my passwords to reflect my quit date several months in advance.

As a management consultant, I got to visit lots of different cubicle farms. Walking into any cube farm is depressing. Approaching the door, I could feel a heavy energy and a sense of dread. The carpets reeked of spilled coffee and powdered donuts. When sitting in a grey and beige cubicle, I'd set down my coffee, pop open my laptop, and enter my password — the one that would remind me of my future job, the one where I'm the boss, and I never need to sit in a grey room ever again. *Oh yeah, this is temporary and only a step toward where I want to go. Keep moving.*

Some might call this magical thinking, but now I know I was really training my unconscious mind.

I also think the woo can get a bad rap. You have to keep your head in the game no matter how hard shit is splattering on the fan. There's no need to call this part magic. This is simply whatever you need to do to keep yourself sane and moving forward, one step at a time.

I can manifest my next paycheck. If I do a certain number of steps like networking with some new people, asking for referrals, writing a bunch of proposals, then I know I'll probably land a new client — and increase the chances of that paycheck. As a copywriter, if I had ten consults, I'll usually end up working with at least half of them. The other half — maybe not a great fit or they weren't ready. I know that new business doesn't come in by putting up a website, then sitting back and doing nothing.

I no longer call my intuition "woo-woo" — doing so only leads to sideways looks and implies that listening to your gut is weird. And it's not. Trusting ourselves is so completely normal; we've only been conditioned to think that it's not.

The language you use toward going after your dream is crucial — and that includes the words you use out loud, write on the page, and think in your head.

Here are some examples. Instead of thinking, "I'm never going to get that job, they won't like me." Try on, "I'm going to show up and give this interview everything I've got. I'm excited to tell them about my awesomeness."

Instead of, "I'm going to be broke forever," you could say, "I'm going to find some ways to make more money, or even start a business on the side."

Instead of, "I'm so tired, I never get enough sleep," try telling yourself, "I'm getting exactly the amount of sleep I need," then get off your butt and go for a walk around the block.

Superstitions and magic might very well be our way of trying to control situations that we could never have control over. We may as well just sit around and smile at everything going on around us. We can't control the outcome, so we can sit back, crack open a cold one, and enjoy the front seats on the show called life.

And especially, if you have to follow a ritual like touching your crystals and sageing every inch of your home before it'll be "clean" and this comes from a place of fear, you might be missing the point. The second that doing a thing or not doing a thing happens because of fear, it's time to pause and evaluate whether this practice is serving you or you're serving the practice. Are the rituals helping you tap into your intuition so that you can make decisions with more confidence?

If so, sage away. But then decide what you want, get to work, and make some changes.

Un-random acts of gratitude

You get what you get, and you don't have a fit. This is timeless wisdom we all heard in elementary school. This, in its purest form, is about wanting less and being okay with what you have.

I have a gratitude practice. When someone says this to you, does it leave you scratching your head? What in the world is a gratitude "practice?" And why do we feel the need to formalize these kinds of things and give them a name?

Gratitude is about being thankful for what you have.

I know you don't want to be one of those jerks who walks around all day complaining about your stuff. *This gigantic house is so much to clean, this pool is way too big, this oversized backyard is such a pain in the ass, all this cooking of this local, organic food is taking way too much time.*

When you invest your time and energy focusing on what you don't want or what you don't have, here's what you'll create — less of what you actually want. This is about wanting what you have instead of wishing for what you don't have.

A simple gratitude practice might include writing down just three things a day you're grateful for. I keep a one-line-a-day, five-year journal to track these moments. Or you could say them out loud or think about what you're grateful for starting with the moment you wake up each morning. No matter how tired you are.

Thanks for letting me wake up in this warm bed with this cool fan running over my body. Simple enough. And it's a much more serving thought than, "Holy crap, I'm exhausted — I need more sleep." Or even, "I have so much to do today, how am I going to do it all?"

Get into the habit of making a simple thank you part of your every day. It doesn't need to be dramatic, and it can be private. I promise if you start saying thanks for the stuff you have, you'll begin to feel a little happier, and you'll start noticing that more of what you do want is coming your way.

At the end of each day, I ask the kids, "What was the best part about your day?" If the kids are pissed about me making them go to bed before they could finish watching TV, they'll angrily respond, "Nothing." Sometimes I have to dig. I usually start by telling them the best parts of my day to get their gratitude wheels turning. *I really enjoyed the work I did today or watching you play or eating dinner with you and talking about school.*

When you lead with gratitude, others will follow.

Those negative nellies in your life that can't seem to do anything but complain — try to kill 'em with kindness (not literally, of course) or wash them in gratitude. When they can't help but complain about all the snow or rain, you can respond and say you just love how nice it looks, or watching it fall is so lovely, or it looks like a holiday card.

Those people will get the point that you're not the one to whine to. They'll either move on to someone else to share their vinegar with or they'll come around. Either way, you can expect to hear less complaining. And when you hear less complaining, you'll probably complain less too. It's a wonderful cycle.

It can be hard to find gratitude in the moments of being in the ditch or when life hands you a crap sandwich and expects you to be happy with what you got. There's probably something in there that can feel good — the hard part might be finding it. If you can make a practice of looking at external events from a place of curiosity — wondering, *How is this me?* and *How is this a reflection of something that's coming up for me to work on?* — you'll find out how experiences are happening *for* you and not *to* you.

Saying thank you more often will fill your thank bank and make you happier.

If you're not used to offering words of appreciation to others, start with yourself. Say thank you for things you might normally grumble about: like the rainy weather or the accident that caused traffic to back up and make you thirty minutes late. Thank you, rainy weather, you saved me from feeling guilty about not walking the dog today. Because it's raining, I got to stay cozy and dry under this fluffy blanket. Thank you, highway accident, for giving me an extra thirty minutes to listen to an audiobook I was really enjoying.

One afternoon, I spent ninety minutes driving ten miles to Talia's gymnastics class. Traffic was so bad we never even made it. I had to turn around and head home, missing the class altogether. Ninety minutes of life I'll never get back.

I was super-mad at first, dropping all the F-bombs in all the places, tense and barely breathing.

When I pulled onto our street, I wanted to rage because there were two cars in front of me driving twenty miles per hour. Do you know how slow twenty miles per hour is? It's crawling. If I could have passed them, I would have. When I finally got past them, I zoomed down the street and pulled into the driveway in haste.

It was only 5:30 p.m. If I continued the rest of the night like this, I was sure to have a crappy night, and it would affect the kids and Ryan too. I turned the car off, took a huge deep breath, and said to the kids, "At least you guys got to watch an extra hour of TV," pointing at the TV in the truck.

"We've been in the car for an hour?" they responded. They

didn't even realize it took so long. I was the only one who was having a problem. While Talia was upset about missing gymnastics, we'd make the class up. And all she wanted to know was if we had time to watch TV at home and have a snack before bed. They were fine. It was all in my head. I turned it around and was happy to have listened to a few good podcast episodes.

Of course, thanking yourself and the universe or whatever you want to call it is important. But if you can leave little love notes of gratitude for others, you'll genuinely brighten someone's day.

Think about leaving a little love note for your mail carrier. Not *that* kind of love note — you don't want them knocking on your door with a big red bow. But just a little "Thank you for bringing my mail" can go a long way.

A little thank you note to the housekeeper who turned down your hotel room all week.

A handwritten sticky note for your partner who's been working long hours lately without much of a break.

A few words of thanks in an email to the blogger who wrote something that touched your soul.

A quick reply on social media to the podcaster who dropped a wise bomb that changed everything.

A letter of praise to the author who inspired you to take action (finally) on something you'd been meaning to do forever.

You never know how your words of gratitude may land. You could change someone's entire day. They might have been sitting there before they heard from you wondering if anyone was reading (besides their mother), wondering what the whole point was. And then your seemingly insignificant little note arrived and changed everything.

You never know how your kind words might touch or inspire someone. It only takes a few minutes.

Leave a glowing online review for your favorite restaurant or send the manager a personal email. There are probably so many things you enjoy every day, and finding a small way to say thank you (reviews help businesses!) can stretch those good vibes even further.

Even if the only thanks you can muster up is for the man who lets you go first in the grocery store lineup or to the barista serving up your Americano. All it takes is to look up for just a second, acknowledge another being, look them in the eyes, and say thank you.

It says, *I see you, I notice you, and I appreciate you.*

Another fun game I like to play is to leave what I call "abundance bombs" in random public places. A single or a five-dollar bill by the sink in the public bathroom, tucked into a library book, or under a candle in a busy cafe for some lucky unsuspecting person to find.

When the kids see me reach for my wallet in a restroom, they know what I'm up to. They love being the ones to help hide the money in plain sight for an unsuspecting hand-washer. (See, it pays to keep your hands clean.)

Sure, we all have our low moments and might find this whole gratitude thing annoying. When you make it a daily habit, however small to start, you will start to notice more things to be grateful for. Good things beget more good things.

They knew it all along, but I finally woke up

Heading to a live event in San Diego one January, I was feeling fuzzy. I didn't quite know what was next in my work. I had declared two main business goals, and other than that, I was feeling pretty open to what the year would bring.

I'd replaced my corporate income in a little over a year of going full time in my business. Naturally, when I hit that goal, I turned my focus to "what's next?"

Openness to what's in front of us is always a good idea, so that wasn't the problem — it was the lack of focus and clarity. I packed my carry-on luggage, hugged my family, and hopped on a plane from Chicago to San Diego, heading to an event on growing your business and to meet some other badass business owners.

What happened next was a series of connections and synchronicities that gave me a new kind of clarity.

All the speakers at the event were amazing. It was the last one who blew my mind in a completely different kind of way. An intuitive consultant took the mic. I knew she was going to talk to us about learning how to use intuition in our businesses. Rad. I love this stuff. And my biz needs *something*.

She took the front of the room with grace, and I was really

excited to learn more from her. She had an energy about her that was magnetic. I'd really wanted to say hi and get to know more about her throughout the event, but every time she caught my eye, she had a small crowd around her.

Obviously, I wasn't the only one drawn to her.

During her chat, she talked about how we feel it in our bodies when we know something is right or wrong for us. After a brief grounding exercise, she asked us all to stand up, ask ourselves a question, and then notice if we naturally lean forward or backward.

You can practice this by saying your name, noticing if your body leans forward or if you feel an upward pull (up or forward mean yes), and then saying your name is something else and noticing if you lean back or feel a downward pull (back or down mean no). Before you do this, clear your mind and stay open to what comes up.

When she opened up to questions, I had a nagging question burning inside me that I was kind of afraid to ask. When I sensed that the time was almost up, I shot my hand up. I had to know.

"How do I know the voices in my head are telling me the right thing to do or the wrong thing to do? And when I can sense things, how do I know if that's my intuition or something else like fear talking?"

Without missing a beat, she told me that I experience it that way because I'm claircognizant. I nodded in the moment, totally clueless, and later Googled it. I learned that it's someone who simply knows things about the future. Cognizance means knowledge or awareness and so claircognizants have the psychic intuition of clear thinking. Intuition shows up differently for everyone. For me, it feels like an obvious knowing. It's now my favorite business and writing tool. I had previously thought that clairvoyant (clear seeing) was the only form of intuition.

She recommended I read a certain book. When she said the title, I froze. I later found out there were a few "no way's!"

echoed throughout the room from the people I had just talked about the book with.

The book she mentioned — *The Untethered Soul* by Michael Singer — had come up four times that same week. I'd already read it once: this was the book left by the previous owners of our house, the one I read in 2014 at the Vegas pool and realized it was time to change my diet from vegan to not vegan. Earlier that week, one of my business mentors recommended it. A mastermind sister and friend mentioned it the day we flew into San Diego, and it had already come up for *her* a few times that week. In my bedroom at our Airbnb for the week, that same book was front and center on the bookshelf.

I had taken a photo of it sitting on the shelf on the day we arrived to show my mentor and friend who was just talking about it. When I found it in the room, I thought it was funny, and wondered if maybe I should reread it.

So when the intuitive suggested this book, my neck got tight and I felt like I could barely breathe. When she was finished answering my question, I had to tell her. She didn't seem at all surprised that the book was popping up all over the place. I downloaded the audio version of the book that evening to listen to on the plane ride home.

Then, she suggested that practicing some channeled writing would be helpful for me. I figured she had noticed me talking about writing at some point over the past two days, so I wasn't surprised, but the faces around me were wide-eyed. And it turned out she really didn't know that I was, in fact, a writer.

The next day, I wanted to track her down to ask her one last question. It was a question that had been on my mind since the summer. I'd never really had an answer to it, so I left it alone — knowing the answer would present itself when the time was right.

This was the last day of the event, and especially after her talk, every time I'd look for her, there were people around her. Some would follow her out of the room because they had questions for her. I didn't overhear many of the questions, but when we finally locked eyes, she pointed at me and said, "We need to talk."

She knew it.

I told her what I'd been contemplating for almost a year.

In the past year, at least a dozen or so healing, energetic, or intuitive types came into my world. Either they were new friends or clients, or they had actually been there all along and I never really noticed. More and more clients that past year had energy or spiritual work at their core.

I asked her, "Why are all these healers, light-workers, and energy workers finding me and wanting to work with me?"

Again, not missing a beat, she answered, "Because they know you're intuitive too."

Spinning, everything seemed to make sense now.

At the end of the event, I packed up my pages of notes, head filled with inspiration and heart exploding with gratitude, knowing without a doubt that it was time to stop hiding it. The knowing. Clients, no matter their industry — healer, tech, health care, designer, performer — all say things to me like, "How'd you get inside my head?" "I don't know how you did it." "It's like you know me."

I'll include pieces of people's stories in their website copy that make them cry — you'd be surprised how often this happens.

I revisit something I wrote — for myself or a client and say, "Oh, I really love that." And then my client says, "You should, you wrote it." You see, I don't remember. I used to think I had a memory problem, but more accurately, it's intuition or my muse — and I forget the details.

Of course, I do very practical things with all my copywriting and coaching clients. We chat on video first to make sure we're both a great fit for working together, sign legal agreements, accept deposits, and go through a thorough (and also, I'm told, really fun) questionnaire.

Once the practical part is there, I marry that with a knowing. I listen to my gut and take risks based on hunches. I stay fully present to what I'm hearing, seeing, and sensing in these moments. Sometimes clients love it, sometimes they don't. That part is beyond my control and it's all okay.

I had been afraid to declare it to my little citrine-lined corner of the internet out of fear of being judged and labeled. I didn't want to be called woo, a hippie, witchy, or whatever label you want to give it, even though I embraced every single one of my clients who might describe themselves this way.

But now, I'm finally declaring it.

I am intuitive.

And *pssst* — you are too.

I write with my intuition. It's one of my writing tools.

When I was around twelve, I recall my mom taking me to a psychic fair inside a hotel ballroom. I don't recall many details about the event or why we were there — I only remember two things about that day:

A strange feeling that everyone was reading my mind as I walked past the booths with palm readers, psychics, and mediums. I made sure to keep my thoughts clean.

And a palm reader taking my hands in hers, studying my palms, and telling me that I had "healing hands." She asked me if my hands got hot around people. And I thought, "Well, yeah, just being around other humans often makes my palms sweat."

And that was it. The only encounter that stood out to me that some would describe as "mystic." That, and I see 11:11 *all the time*.

It only took me hearing it, then reconfirming it from many, many others, before I could feel even remotely comfortable attaching it to my name. One day on a whim several months ago, I added it to my website copy in a not-so-obvious spot and didn't tell anyone. Slowly, over time, I've gotten cozier with the word, sprinkling it into my email signature, social media profiles, and calling those nudges what they are — my intuition.

Here's how the clear knowing shows up for me:

When shit hits the fan, and I'm being walked out of a job, I know — it's okay.

When we are house hunting and I know without a doubt which ones are wrong, and which ones are right — merely by standing on the sidewalk.

When I'm on a consult call with a potential client, and I get the urge to sit and talk to them all day, or run, I know.

When I dream about someone, and they show up in my inbox the next day.

When I'm hosting a writing marathon, looking at some copy, and serving up some helpful feedback, and for some reason, I get stuck reading a few seemingly benign words over and over. I *know* there's something more in there that needs to come out, and sometimes I can't pinpoint what it is. I just hang out there, looking at it until I get a nudge. Sometimes it's prompting someone to go deeper, or I'll ask a question. And when I don't know, I say, "Tell me more about this," to see what comes up from there. Often, I strike a nerve.

When I'm reading something or listening to someone tell me something, and I get a very distinct tingly feeling. It creeps down the right side of my neck from behind my ear to my shoulder — like someone walking their fingertips across my neck. And then I know — pay attention, Jacq — there's something here for you. If you're wondering if you have intuition, you do. It took until I was almost forty to be able to articulate it.

I ignored those intuitive nudges for so long it's a wonder that they kept showing up to poke me. Well, I'm sure glad they did. *Thank you for not giving up on me!*

It showed up when we first went into early 2020 business, and my chest was tight, and I felt like I might have been having a heart attack. I realized I was taking on everyone else's fear and pain. That chest tightness didn't belong to me. I confirmed this because I was able to let it go so quickly.

A knowing is sometimes clunky and awkward to explain to people.

I get lots of deer-in-headlights looks — I'm okay with this now. I have to trust it. And when I share my insights with clients, I always ask permission — or they've asked me first, and I respond. Many of my clients have a finely tuned intuition too, so they know how to listen and trust their inner knowing.

Sometimes I open my mouth, and words fall out — it's like they're not even mine. This is something I have to be careful of. Many times people have said to me, "You said this and this," and, confused, I'm trying to recall — "I did? Are you sure?"

Sometimes I ask questions that feel uncomfortable, and that discomfort is often not mine. It's up to the person on the receiving end to decide what to do with it.

And I think this is part of the reason why I initially held back on associating with the word intuitive: because I want to encourage people to discover their truth — not tell them what to do. I know that my clients know the answer, and sometimes they don't see it right away. I want them to find the answers for themselves, so that they can learn to trust their intuition too — and they all have it.

This is a special kind of intuitive coaching dance because sometimes I share an idea, and that's what they needed to hear. Sometimes a question doesn't bring up anything at all — and we hear crickets. These are all perfectly okay.

It took me a long time to learn the language of my intuition.

I'm still figuring it all out, but one thing's for sure — it's getting sharper the more I pay attention.

Outro

Thank you for riding along next to me through these changes. My greatest hope is that you simply notice just how much you've changed — over the course of your life, the past year, and even since you began reading this book.

I have an intuitive nudge that you're in one of two places:

One, you are embracing all your beautiful life changes. You're proud of how you've handled them and grateful for the lessons they've brought — the intentional changes and the surprising ones.

Or, two — there's a pang in your gut that's craving change. You know that something needs to change. Maybe it feels like you're stuck. You need to do something — but what? How do you choose?

I understand because I was there. My greatest wish for you is that you start. Taking one small step is how you create change. And then another, and another.

You know how it feels to adapt to an unwanted change with the flip of a script.

You've practiced resiliency.

Bit by bit, one experience at a time, we'll discover all the things that matter most to us.

Scrolling social media for four hours — doesn't matter.

Complaining without choosing change — doesn't matter.

Following a schedule to the minute — doesn't matter.

Freaking out — doesn't matter.

Getting mad at all the people who aren't doing their part — doesn't matter.

Playing Scrabble after dinner — matters.

Discovering our values and making choices in line with our values — matters.

Creating an impact — matters.

Choosing good company — matters.

Being present for others and for ourselves — matters.

Sometimes change isn't always necessary. We often think we need a change when really we just need to stick to the thing we've been doing.

On the opposite end of people who are afraid of change and avoid it like a root canal are the people who crave constant change. How can they ever get bored if they're constantly changing jobs, books, focus, projects? How many unfinished projects do you need to rack up before you realize you need to spend some time being okay with being in your skin?

You may be staring down the barrel of a significant change, wondering if it's a necessary one.

Start here. Will this change make your life better? Is it good for you? Is it good for your family and friends? Is it good for society?

Or do you continue doing the same? Remember, doing nothing is a decision too.

The unfussy life is about choosing change when it matters.

You might want to turn around and go back to where it's safe now. Change can feel scary. You might want to run back to familiar territory — where you know the game and all the players.

At the end of your life, will you say, "I'm happy I played it safe and stayed as comfortable as possible and avoided change?"

Or will you stand proud, knowing you figured out what you value, stood up for what you believed in, even when it was uncomfortable, and chose necessary change?

When the people who aren't your people have something to say — and they will — all you can do is smile. Excuse yourself from the table and find a new one to pull up to.

This journey through change we call life holds so many lessons for us.

What matters to you tomorrow might be different than what matters today.

Today was uncertain anyway. Tomorrow is uncertain too — always has been.

Be here. Be in your life. Be the person you're proud of while you make changes in your life for the better.

Sometimes I wonder if I did things the hard way. Taking the long path to figure out the best way to do things and make stuff happen. Getting laid off three times before I finally took a clue; moving states, then countries before finding home; trying different kinds of work before landing on work I love. And this may all change again too.

This is why we write books and read books, isn't it? So we can save ourselves the pain and suffering that someone else went through. BUT... does it really work that way? I think it's an illusion. A book can take you on someone else's journey, and in so doing it can clarify your own path — but you still have to walk it, right?

I hope you found delight in this book. I hope you enjoyed the journey — questioning some of your practices along the way. I hope that it reminded you to open the good wine.

I hope this book brought you peace. A reminder that you're doing okay — you're doing more than enough, every single day, doing everything you want to do.

I hope this book gave you permission to stop trying to hold everything up. Permission to take back control of your life and make conscious choices.

And maybe it has you thinking about a change you'd like to make. Perhaps you're ready for it now.

I hope it feels like coming home.

Swinging open the heavy rustic wood door to an unfussy life.

Gratitude

With a big beautiful book project that took three years from the time I first sat down at my desk with a wild idea for a book, to reshaping it over and over, there are lots of people I'd love to thank.

First, Ryan. Thank you for putting up with me while I was on this rollercoaster ride.

Jacob, for teaching me about integrity, and perseverance, and determination.

Talia, for reminding me that I am, in fact, creative. Thank you for your big, beautiful, outspoken heart.

My mom and dad for giving me the best childhood one could hope for.

My sister, Jen, for challenging me and being there — no matter what.

For my mastermind sisters, who encourage me to keep dreaming bigger — and to trust, allow, and surrender.

For my editor, Kristen Tate, who took this rough pile of words and spun them into word gold.

For my designer, Elizabeth Cooper, artist and intuitive coach, who poured pure magic into this gorgeous cover.

And finally, to my guides, my higher self, for allowing these words to fall out when I sit alone with a blank page and blinking cursor.

Epilogue

Let's close this out with an unfussy life manifesto.

I believe…

> In not giving a fuck
> In giving a fuck
> In saying no
> That you're influenced by the people you spend time with
> That you matter
> That gossip makes us small
> In constant growth
> In being better than you were yesterday
> That doing work you love matters — maybe more than you think
> That details matter
> In looking at the big picture
> In being honest
> In being real and genuine and true
> In the simple life
> In buying less shit

In unplugging
In spending more time with people than screens
In knowing someone's eye color before knowing what
 they had for lunch
In deciding
In choosing
In changing
Always changing

About the Author

Jacqueline Fisch is a copywriter, intuitive writing coach and founder of The Intuitive Writing School. She helps writers make progress on their passion projects and creative business owners sound more human in their writing.

Before launching her writing and coaching business, Jacq spent 13 years working in corporate communications and management-consulting for clients including Fortune 500 companies and the US government. As a freelance copywriter, she's helped hundreds of clients – tech startups, life and business coaches, creatives, and more – learn how to communicate more authentically and stand out in a busy online world.

After bouncing around with two passports between Toronto and a handful of states, she's decided that home is where the people are. She finds home with her husband, two kids, a dog, a cat, a few houseplants hanging on by a thread, and most of her sanity. If you show up for a visit, she'll definitely get out the good wine.

Connect with Jacq at www.theintuitivewritingschool.com

About The Intuitive Writing School Community

An online writing community for creatives who want accountability, support, and authentic resources to tell their stories.

I founded The Intuitive Writing School Community to help creative business owners sound human in their online copy and give writers the time and space to finish their creative projects.

While I initially created this community for others, it turned out to be what I needed to finish this book.

Even though I supported entrepreneurs with their writing every day, my writing kept falling to the bottom of my to-do list — days and, eventually, months passed while this project sat untouched.

The world needs your words too. Whatever writing project is on your heart, I invite you to join this sacred container and get the support you need to finish. Learn more and join us at https://theintuitivewritingschool.com/community

I'm excited to write with you,
Jacq xo

www.ingramcontent.com/pod-product-compliance
Lightning Source LLC
Chambersburg PA
CBHW070044230426
43661CB00005B/755

9781736554203